Thurgood Marshall

These and other titles are included in The Importance
Of biography series:

Alexander the Great	Harry Houdini
Muhammad Ali	Thomas Jefferson
Louis Armstrong	Mother Jones
James Baldwin	Chief Joseph
Clara Barton	Joe Louis
Napoleon Bonaparte	Malcolm X
Julius Caesar	Thurgood Marshall
Rachel Carson	Margaret Mead
Charlie Chaplin	Michelangelo
Charlemagne	Wolfgang Amadeus Mozart
Cesar Chavez	John Muir
Winston Churchill	Sir Isaac Newton
Cleopatra	Richard M. Nixon
Christopher Columbus	Georgia O'Keeffe
Hernando Cortes	Louis Pasteur
Marie Curie	Pablo Picasso
Amelia Earhart	Elvis Presley
Thomas Edison	Jackie Robinson
Albert Einstein	Norman Rockwell
Duke Ellington	Anwar Sadat
Dian Fossey	Margaret Sanger
Benjamin Franklin	Oskar Schindler
Galileo Galilei	John Steinbeck
Emma Goldman	Tecumseh
Jane Goodall	Jim Thorpe
Martha Graham	Mark Twain
Stephen Hawking	Queen Victoria
Jim Henson	Pancho Villa
Adolf Hitler	H. G. Wells

Thurgood Marshall

by
Deborah Hitzeroth and Sharon Leon

Lucent Books, P.O. Box 289011, San Diego, CA 92198-9011

Library of Congress Cataloging-in-Publication Data

Hitzeroth, Deborah, 1961–
    Thurgood Marshall / by Deborah Hitzeroth and
      Sharon Leon.
      p.   cm. — (The importance of)
    Includes bibliographical references and index.
    Summary: Presents the life and legacy of the first African
American Supreme Court justice.
    ISBN 1-56006-061-1 (alk. paper)
    1. Marshall, Thurgood, 1908–1993—Juvenile literature.
    2. Judges—United States—Biography—Juvenile literature.
    3. Afro-American judges—United States—Biography—
Juvenile literature.   4. United States. Supreme Court—
Biography—Juvenile literature. [1. Marshall, Thurgood,
1908–1993. 2. Lawyers. 3. Judges. 4. Afro-Americans—
Biography.] I. Leon, Sharon, 1959–   . II. Title. III. Series.
KF8745.M34H58   1997
347.73'2634—dc21   96–40129
[B]   CIP
                                                     AC

Copyright 1997 by Lucent Books, Inc., P.O. Box 289011,
San Diego, California 92198-9011

Printed in the U.S.A.

Contents

Foreword

THE IMPORTANCE OF biography series deals with individuals who have made a unique contribution to history. The editors of the series have deliberately chosen to cast a wide net and include people from all fields of endeavor. Individuals from politics, music, art, literature, philosophy, science, sports, and religion are all represented. In addition, the editors did not restrict the series to individuals whose accomplishments have helped change the course of history. Of necessity, this criterion would have eliminated many whose contribution was great, though limited. Charles Darwin, for example, was responsible for radically altering the scientific view of the natural history of the world. His achievements continue to impact the study of science today. Others, such as Chief Joseph of the Nez Percé, played a pivotal role in the history of their own people. While Joseph's influence does not extend much beyond the Nez Percé, his nonviolent resistance to white expansion and his continuing role in protecting his tribe and his homeland remain an inspiration to all.

These biographies are more than factual chronicles. Each volume attempts to emphasize an individual's contributions both in his or her own time and for posterity. For example, the voyages of Christopher Columbus opened the way to European colonization of the New World. Unquestionably, his encounter with the New World brought monumental changes to both Europe and the Americas in his day. Today, however, the broader impact of Columbus's voyages is being critically scrutinized. *Christopher Columbus,* as well as every biography in The Importance Of series, includes and evaluates the most recent scholarship available on each subject.

Each author includes a wide variety of primary and secondary source quotations to document and substantiate his or her work. All quotes are footnoted to show readers exactly how and where biographers derive their information, as well as provide stepping stones to further research. These quotations enliven the text by giving readers eyewitness views of the life and times of each individual covered in The Importance Of series.

Finally, each volume is enhanced by photographs, bibliographies, chronologies, and comprehensive indexes. For both the casual reader and the student engaged in research, The Importance Of biographies will be a fascinating adventure into the lives of people who have helped shape humanity's past and present, and who will continue to shape its future.

Important Dates in the Life of Thurgood Marshall

1908

Thurgood Marshall is born to William and Norma Marshall in Baltimore, Maryland.

1930

Marshall receives his bachelor's degree from Lincoln University; is denied entrance to the University of Maryland Law School because he is an African American.

1931

Is accepted at Howard University, where he meets his mentor, Charles Houston. Begins classes at Howard in September 1931.

1933

Graduates from Howard University Law School and begins working with the NAACP in Baltimore.

1935

Files and wins lawsuit against the University of Maryland Law School on behalf of Donald Murray, thus succeeding in desegregating the law school.

1936

Takes position of assistant special counsel for the NAACP in New York City.

1938

Takes Houston's place as chief legal counsel of the NAACP.

1940

Becomes director of the NAACP's Legal Defense and Education Fund.

1952

Begins arguments on *Brown v. Board of Education* before the U.S. Supreme Court.

1954

Supreme Court's ruling on *Brown v. Board of Education* ends legalized segregation in public schools.

1962

Marshall is appointed U.S. Court of Appeals judge.

1965

President Lyndon B. Johnson names Marshall solicitor general of the United States.

1967

President Johnson appoints Marshall to the Supreme Court; Marshall becomes the first African American to serve on the Court.

1968

Marshall writes his first majority opinion for the Court in the case of *Interstate Circuit, Inc. v. City of Dallas*, involving freedom-of-speech issues.

1972

Writes a stinging dissent in the case of *Adams v. Williams*, which allows police officers to stop and search suspects.

1991

Retires from the Supreme Court.

1993

Dies of heart failure at the National Naval Medical Center in Bethesda, Maryland.

Mr. Civil Rights

America has been plagued with discrimination and racism during most of its history. Less than fifty years ago laws existed that kept African Americans and Caucasians separated, or segregated, from each other. These laws also prohibited African Americans from owning property and enjoying many of the civil rights guaranteed to all Americans by the U.S. Constitution.

These laws were changed through the labor of men and women dedicated to working for civil rights for African Americans. One of the leaders was Thurgood Marshall, a man who dedicated his entire life to striking down unjust laws and winning social equality for all Americans.

Marshall, the great-grandson of a slave, grew up in the South and experienced racism and discrimination firsthand. When he was young, many of the boundaries of his life were set by the color of his skin. Because he was an African American, he could not shop in the same

Thurgood Marshall, a powerful voice in the struggle to end segregation, fought to overturn the laws that allowed racism in America.

stores, sit in the same section of the bus, or even attend the same schools as white children. And even though he was an honor student in college, Marshall was refused admission to the University of Maryland school of law because the university would not accept black students.

It was these types of experiences and the discrimination he saw others experience that made him a staunch fighter for social justice. In fact Marshall spent so much of his life fighting for racial equality that he earned the nickname Mr. Civil Rights.

Marshall earned the title through six decades of work for African-American civil rights. During this time Marshall fought to establish equality in education and for black U.S. military personnel, as well as for equal rights before the law for all Americans. Marshall also distinguished himself as the United States' first black solicitor general and the first black justice to serve on the Supreme Court.

Marshall believed deeply in the words inscribed above the front entrance of the Supreme Court Building, "Equal justice under the law." Marshall spent his life trying to ensure that those words were true. His work left an indelible mark upon America. In a 1992 interview quoted by Marshall biographer D. J. Herda, former Chief Justice Warren E. Burger said of Marshall, "I find it difficult to identify a single individual in the legal profession who has done more to advance the cause of civil rights in this century than Thurgood Marshall."[1]

Chapter

1 Shaping a Leader

When Thurgood Marshall was born in 1908, America was a difficult place for African Americans, who often faced discrimination and persecution. More than three decades had passed since President Abraham Lincoln had issued the Emancipation Proclamation, which ended slavery in the United States, but segments of white society had yet to change their racial attitudes.

Many states had passed segregation laws designed to keep white and black Americans separate. The laws were often called Jim Crow laws after an unflattering song made popular by a white New York actor. Jim Crow laws prevented African Americans from voting, owning property, or running for office in many states. The laws also mandated that most public places had to be segregated, or divided into separate areas for blacks and whites. Because of these laws blacks were denied service in stores, hotels, and restaurants. African Americans had to enter banks and public buildings through separate entrances, had to sit in what was called the colored section on buses and trains, and had to use separate restrooms, waiting rooms, and drinking fountains.

Segregation was present in every aspect of American society. "In courtrooms, . . . black lawyers were exceedingly rare and black judges nonexistent," writes author John Egerton in his book *Speak Now Against the Day*. "Hospitals where black doctors and nurses could not practice

Before the passage of civil rights laws in the 1960s, most public places were segregated. Here, a black man and a white boy in a southern town drink from separate fountains labeled "colored" and "white."

A Mississippi theatergoer climbs the stairs that lead to a separate, back entrance for black patrons. Such segregation was common throughout much of Marshall's life.

denied admission to black patients. . . . There were jobs and unions and even entire industries that catered to one race or the other, but not both. Cemeteries were either black or white."[2]

Discrimination and violence against blacks was also common. Throughout the South there were cases of black defendants being lynched by mobs before they had a chance to stand trial and instances of black business owners being beaten and driven from their homes by throngs of white racists. Usually the perpetrators of these crimes went unpunished.

Reporter Ida B. Wells-Barnett, a former slave and crusader for African-American rights, spoke out against the conditions she saw in the South during the early 1900s. She notes, "In one section, at least of our common country, a government of the people, by the people, and for the people means a government by the mob."[3]

A Strong Family

This was the world into which Thurgood Marshall was born on July 2, 1908, in Baltimore, Maryland. Growing up, Marshall heard many stories of how his family had fought discrimination. In later life, Marshall attributed his fighting spirit to his family. One of his favorite stories was about his great-grandfather, who was brought to the United States as a slave in the 1840s. Marshall's great-grandfather refused to accept his role as a slave and refused to submit to his owner's orders. Finally his owner gave up the fight and freed him. Recounting his great-grandfather's release, Marshall explained:

> One day his owner came up to him and said, "Look, I brought you here so I guess I can't very well shoot you—as you deserve. On the other hand, I can't with a clear conscience sell anyone as vicious as you to another slave holder, and I can't give you away. So, I am going to set you free—on one condition. Get . . . out of this county and never come back."[4]

Even after he was freed, Marshall's great-grandfather refused to follow orders. Instead of leaving the county, he settled down a few miles from his former owner's plantation and lived there until he died. This fighting spirit continued with Marshall's grandfather, Thoroughgood, also a former slave, who fought in the Civil War with the Union army. Marshall used another of his favorite stories about his grandmother, Annie, to illustrate his family's stubborn streak.

According to the story, the Baltimore Gas and Electric Company planned to install a light pole in front of the Marshalls' grocery store, and Annie was furious. She believed the sidewalk in front of her store belonged to her and that she had the right to decide how her property would be used. And she did not want a pole stuck in the middle of her sidewalk, blocking the view of her store. When workers arrived to install the light, they found Annie sitting in a chair directly over the spot on which they were supposed to install the pole. Unable to get her to move, the workers left. The men came back three more days, and each time they found Annie blocking their path. Finally the electric company gave up and found a new spot for their light. Telling the story later, Thurgood said, "Grandma Annie emerged as the victor of what may have been the first successful sit down strike in Maryland."[5]

Marshall also received some of his rebellious nature from his mother's family. In the 1870s his maternal grandfather, Isaiah Williams, helped organize large public

There Is No Freedom in a Land Where Mobs Rule

In The Eyes on the Prize Civil Rights Reader, *edited by Clayborne Carson and others, Ida B. Wells-Barnett describes her experiences with discrimination.*

"In one section, at least of our common country, a government of the people, by the people, and for the people means a government by the mob; where the land of the free and the home of the brave means a land of lawlessness, murder and outrage and where liberty of speech means the license of might to destroy the businesses and drive from home those who exercise this privilege contrary to the will of the mob."

Growing up, Thurgood heard many stories about his family's fighting spirit, which, he says, inspired him to fight against racial discrimination as an adult.

family lived in West Baltimore in a middle-class neighborhood where white and black families lived in peaceful integration.

Norma, an elementary school teacher in one of Baltimore's segregated schools, had attended college and graduate school. Thurgood's mother believed her two sons needed a good education and she ensured that Thurgood and his older brother, William Aubrey, were good students. Thurgood's father worked for the Baltimore & Ohio Railroad as a dining-car waiter. This was a prosperous job, and he was able to support his family comfortably.

Although Thurgood's father, William, had not attended college, he was self-educated and a community leader. He loved reading about the law and followed

Thurgood, shown here at about age two, inherited his interest in law from his father, who had a passion for politics and social issues.

meetings to protest police brutality toward blacks in Baltimore. Organizing these meetings was dangerous because groups of white racists beat and sometimes killed black leaders who protested social conditions. Stories about his grandfather's protests proved to Marshall that the black community could be roused to work together for a common cause. It was an example that Marshall would follow later in his life.

Educating a Rebel

Thurgood's sense of social justice was fine-tuned by his parents, Norma Arica and William Canfield Marshall. While most of Baltimore was still segregated, Thurgood's

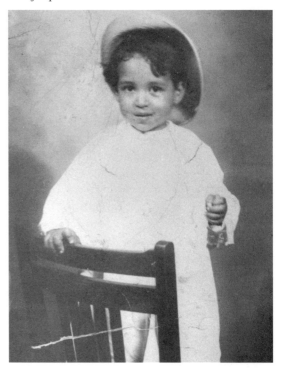

Mobs and Violence

"If [President Abraham] Lincoln could revisit this country in the flesh, he would be disheartened and discouraged. . . . In many states Lincoln would find justice enforced, if at all, by judges elected by one element in a community to pass [judgment] upon the liberties and lives of another. He would see the black men and women, for whose freedom a hundred thousand soldiers gave their lives, set apart in trains, in which they pay first-class fares for third-class service, and segregated in railway stations and in places of entertainment; he would observe that State after State declines to do its elementary duty in preparing the Negro through education for the best exercise of citizenship.

Added to this, the spread of lawless attacks on the Negro, North, South and West—even in the Springfield made famous by Lincoln—often accompanied by revolting brutalities, sparing neither sex nor age nor youth, could but shock the author of the sentiment that 'government of the people, by the people, for the people, should [sic] not perish from the earth.'"

local court cases closely. On his days off he would often take his sons to the local courthouse to watch trials. William served as the first black person on a Baltimore grand jury (a jury that meets to review cases and decide if there is enough evidence to press charges against someone accused of a crime). During his first two days of duty, William noticed that the jury always asked if the person under investigation was white or black. He found that black suspects had charges brought against them more often than white ones. On his third day William requested that the jury no longer be given information about a suspect's race. Surprisingly for the times, the jury's white foreman agreed with William and the grand jury abruptly stopped asking a defendant's race throughout the time William served on the jury.

At home William frequently discussed politics, social issues, and the Constitution with his family. Thurgood and his brother were encouraged to join the discussions, but they were expected to be able to defend their opinions. Later, Marshall credited these family debates with helping him choose a law career. "He [Marshall's father] never told me to become a lawyer, but he turned me into one. He did it by teaching me to argue, by challenging my logic on every point, by making me prove every statement I made."[6]

Thurgood was particularly well equipped for any family debate that centered on the U.S. Constitution. His grade school principal punished anyone caught misbehaving in class by making the disobedient student memorize a passage from the Constitution. Being a high-spirited and mischievous student, Thurgood had ample time to study the document. By the time he graduated from grade school, he had memorized the entire Constitution.

Despite Thurgood's familiarity with the Constitution, part of what he read puzzled him. The words of the Fourteenth Amendment guaranteed equal rights for all citizens. But young Marshall realized that rights as they were written differed from rights as they were applied. Even though he had led a fairly sheltered and privileged life, Thurgood had been exposed to discrimination and prejudice. Even though he came from a well-educated middle-class family, he could not attend the same schools as the white children on his street and he still had to sit in the segregated section of restaurants and theaters. During an interview later in his life, Marshall told a reporter about the day he became aware of racism. It was the first time Marshall had heard anyone use a racial slur, and he realized how wide-ranging racism was.

I heard a kid call a Jewish boy I knew a "kike" to his face. I was about seven. I asked him why he didn't fight the kid. He asked me what would I do if somebody called me "nigger"—would I fight? That was a new one on me. I knew kike was a dirty word, but

Though Thurgood grew up in an integrated neighborhood and led a fairly privileged life, he nevertheless felt the stings of racism as a teenager.

I hadn't known about nigger. I went home and wanted to know right that minute what all this meant. That's not easy for a parent to explain so it makes any sense to a kid, you know.

William Marshall also told his son that if "anyone calls you nigger, you not only got my permission to fight him—you got my orders to fight him."[7]

Once during his adolescence Thurgood had to follow his father's instructions. While in high school Thurgood worked as a delivery boy to raise money for college. One day while balancing a load of boxes so tall he could barely see, Thurgood tried to board a train. Suddenly someone grabbed him and dragged him back to the train platform. As Thurgood later related, the man pulling him from the train called him a nigger and accused him of boarding the train before a white woman who was waiting. Feeling insulted and angry, Thurgood followed his father's advice, and a heated fight ensued. This fistfight would not be the last time Marshall fought racism and bigotry, though in the future he would use a courtroom and the Constitution instead of his fists.

College Years

In 1925 Thurgood graduated from high school and left home for college. Once again he experienced the sting of racism. Even though he was intelligent, there were very few colleges he could attend. Because of segregation most colleges and universities excluded blacks, and there were few institutions available to African Americans seeking higher education.

Marshall, however, enrolled at Lincoln University in Chester, Pennsylvania, the nation's oldest black college. Called the black Princeton, Lincoln educated most of the black leaders of the 1930s and 1940s. Marshall's classmates included Kwame Nkrumah, a future president of Ghana, as well as poet Langston Hughes, who would later become one of the leaders of Harlem's black literary revival in the 1930s.

During his early college years Thurgood was not a very serious student. He was more interested in having fun than in studying, and he delighted in pulling pranks on his fellow students. Still, despite his indifference to his schoolwork, Marshall maintained a B average and pursued a dual major in American literature and philosophy. Through his classes Marshall developed an interest in the works of leading black authors, particularly the writings of W. E. B. Du Bois, a scholar and activist who was known for his essays on the lives of African Americans. Marshall was also

Marshall (second row, second from right) poses with his classmates at Lincoln University, an all-black college in Chester, Pennsylvania.

influenced by Carter Woodson's *The Negro in American History* and Jerome Dowd's *The American Negro.*

Inspired to take action against racism by Du Bois's essays on racism and activism, Marshall took part in his first civil rights protest while at Lincoln. Marshall and twenty-five of his friends went to a theater in a nearby town that had segregated sections for black and white patrons. Marshall's group refused to sit in the black section located in an upper balcony, an area that was not as clean as the rest of the theater and from which it was harder to hear and see the movie. Instead, Marshall's group insisted on sitting in the whites-only orchestra section. Even though some of the white moviegoers snarled insults at them, the group did not move. Marshall wrote of the incident to his parents, saying:

> [We thought] they wouldn't have the nerve or the room in the jail to arrest all of us. But the amazing thing was that when we were leaving, we just walked out with all those other people and they didn't do anything, didn't say anything, didn't even look at us—at least, not as far as I know. I'm not sure I like being invisible, but maybe it's better than being put to shame and not able to respect yourself.[8]

From that night forward, black moviegoers sat where they wanted in that movie theater. It was a small victory to Marshall, but it was his first experience at fighting for social equality.

While at Lincoln, Marshall met Vivian Burey, a student at the nearby University of Pennsylvania. Vivian, called Buster by her friends, and Thurgood quickly fell in love and decided to get married a few years after he graduated. "First we decided to get married five years after I graduated, then three, then one, and we finally did, just before I started my last semester,"[9] Thurgood

A 1937 photograph of a Mississippi movie theater reveals the segregation that existed at the time.

later said of his courtship with Buster. Vivian and Thurgood were married on September 4, 1929. Buster had a stabilizing influence on Marshall and helped him focus more on his schoolwork. The young couple moved into a small apartment, and Marshall devoted himself to completing his last year of school.

His hard work paid off, and Marshall graduated cum laude, with distinction, from Lincoln University in 1930. As he faced graduation, Marshall was still not sure what he wanted to do with his life. Marshall's parents, especially his mother, were urging him to become a dentist. His older brother, William Aubrey, had graduated from Lincoln University in 1926 and then gone on to medical school at Howard University, another all-black institution. With his parents' encouragement, it seemed Thurgood would surely follow in William Aubrey's footsteps and choose a medical career.

But Marshall did not believe medicine was really his calling. His outspokenness had already gotten him into trouble with one premedical studies professor at Lincoln and he had failed that professor's course. Even though he had done well in his other premedical courses, they had not excited him. The only school activity that Marshall was passionate about was the debate team. His friends teased him, saying that he would be the top student in Lincoln's history if he were graded only on debating. After much thought, and with Buster's support, Marshall decided that he should use his debating skills to become a lawyer.

A Student Scorned

Marshall applied to the law school at the University of Maryland in 1930. Even though the University of Maryland was a state university that was supported by taxes from both white and African-American residents, its professional schools, such as law and medicine, were segregated. The university had never accepted a black law student, and those who applied were usually referred to other schools. Even so, Thurgood decided to apply because the school had a good reputation and he thought attending a Maryland law school would best prepare him for practicing law in his home state.

But the university made no exceptions to its policy for Marshall. He received a brusque letter informing him of a nearby school that he should consider attending. The letter read in part that "under the general laws of this State the University maintains the Princess Anne Academy as a separate institution of higher learning for the education of Negroes."[10] The Princess Anne Academy was a junior college staffed with teachers who did not possess college degrees. It was not accredited by the state, and it did not have a law school. Marshall felt furious and powerless, but he refused to give up his desire to become a lawyer.

2 Finding a Calling

Following his humiliating rejection by the University of Maryland, Marshall applied to Howard University in Washington, D.C., the closest law school, an hour away by train, that would admit African Americans. He was immediately accepted and began classes in September 1931.

His first term's schedule at Howard was demanding, but for the first time in his academic career, Marshall felt exhilarated. The law classes fascinated him, and the professors challenged and inspired him. Most inspiring of all was Charles Hamilton Houston, a brilliant lawyer who had graduated in the top 5 percent of his class from Harvard University's law school.

Houston was appointed vice dean of the Howard University Law School in 1929. When he took charge, the law school consisted of little more than a few run-down classrooms filled with old books and staffed by poorly qualified instructors. Most of the law students were

After the University of Maryland denied him admission because of his race, Marshall applied to Howard University, pictured here.

A Friend and an Inspiration

Charles Hamilton Houston was Thurgood Marshall's mentor and lifelong friend. In the following excerpt from Debra Hess's book Thurgood Marshall: The Fight for Equal Justice, *Marshall reminisces about Houston.*

"First off, you thought he was a mean so-and-so. He used to tell us that doctors could bury their mistakes, but lawyers couldn't. And he'd drive home to us that we would be competing not only with white lawyers but really well trained white lawyers, so there just wasn't any point in crying in our beer about being Negroes. And I'll tell you—the going was rough. There must have been thirty of us in that class when we started, and no more than eight or ten of us finished up. He was so tough we used to call him 'Iron Shoes' and 'Cement Pants' and a few other names that don't bear repeating. But he was a sweet man once you saw what he was up to. He was absolutely fair, and the door to his office was always open. He made it clear to all of us that when we were done, we were expected to go out and do something with our lives."

part-time night students. The school was not accredited by the American Bar Association, and the lawyers who graduated from Howard received little respect from their white colleagues.

Houston's task was to bring the law school up to the standards of white law schools. Together with Howard University president Mordecai Johnson, he set about making Howard University's law school the best of its kind in the country. They hired new law professors, bought new books and materials, upgraded the curriculum, and eliminated the night classes to encourage students to devote themselves full-time to their law studies.

Houston pushed his staff hard to bring the law program up to his exacting standards. Within five years the Howard University Law School had achieved full accreditation, recognition from the American Bar Association, and respect for its graduates.

Houston had big plans for the lawyers he was training at Howard. All his life he had chafed under the burden of racism and had come to the conclusion that the best way to fight it was through the legal system. As vice dean of the law school, Houston was able to watch for promising young law students who could lead the way in the fight for equal rights for black Americans. Thurgood Marshall impressed him as a young man who could become one of those leaders.

Cement Pants

Marshall quickly came to respect his ideal-istic law professor. He gave Houston the credit for changing him into a serious stu-dent, saying:

> I never worked hard until I got to the Howard Law School and met Charlie Houston. I saw this man's dedication, his vision, his willingness to sacrifice, and I told myself, "You either shape up or ship out." When you are being chal-lenged by a great human being, you know that you can't ship out.[11]

In addition to presiding over the law school as vice dean, Houston also taught several classes himself, including one on civil rights law. Houston had created the classes to teach his law students how to use the Constitution to obtain equality for African Americans. Marshall discovered that Houston shared his belief that the Constitution promised equal rights for all Americans. Houston told his students it was their job to use the Constitution to make sure African Americans had all the opportunities that other Americans had. He drilled into his students that it was their duty to use their education to recon-struct their communities, to become what he called "social engineers," people who could change, or reengineer, society. Houston was fond of saying that "a lawyer's either a social engineer, or he's a parasite on society."[12]

Marshall found Houston to be a fasci-nating but demanding instructor. Accord-ing to Marshall,

> We called Houston "cement drawers" and "iron shoes" because he banged

As vice dean of Howard University Law School, Charles Hamilton Houston strove to raise the all-black university to the standards of white universities. During Houston's tenure, the law school became accredited by the American Bar Association.

our heads with his belief in dedication. . . . Houston instilled in you the idea that the state, the school, the profes-sors were giving you something for nothing, and that you had to give something back.[13]

Marshall was inspired by Houston's passion and his logic, and Marshall learned from Houston that an African-American lawyer could not just be good, but must be excellent. Marshall recalled years later Houston telling his classes:

When you get in a courtroom, you can't just say, "Please, Mr. Court, have mercy on me because I'm a Negro." You are in competition with a well-trained white lawyer, and you better be at least as good as he is; and if you expect to win, you better be better. If I give you five cases to read overnight, you better read eight. And when I say eight, you read ten. You go that step further, and you might make it.[14]

Marshall took Houston's words to heart and dedicated himself to his studies. Marshall said, "I heard law books

were to dig in so I dug, way deep. I got through simply by overwhelming the job. I was at it twenty hours a day, seven days a week."[15]

Mentor and Friend

Marshall's dedication soon made him one of Houston's favorite students. He often tagged along when Houston attended National Association for the Advancement of Colored People (NAACP) board meetings. The NAACP was organized in 1909 by both white and African-

The National Association for the Advancement of Colored People, founded in 1909, worked to end racial discrimination and to ensure civil rights. Here, young volunteers sort through paperwork in an NAACP office.

American people who were concerned about injustices and violence against African Americans. The NAACP worked to gain civil rights for African Americans, and Houston was an active and enthusiastic member.

Marshall impressed the senior NAACP board members with his energy and intelligence. Executive secretary Walter White spoke highly of Marshall, the

> lanky, brash young senior law student who was always present. I used to wonder at his presence and sometimes was amazed at his assertiveness in challenging positions [taken] by Charlie [Houston] and the other lawyers. But I soon learned of his great value to the cause.[16]

United by a common belief in the Constitution and by a common goal to bring justice to their race, Houston and Marshall forged a friendship that would last throughout their lives. His work with Houston at this time also later led him into a career with the NAACP.

On His Own

In 1933 Thurgood Marshall graduated at the top of his class from Howard University Law School and soon after passed the Maryland State Bar examination, allowing him to practice law. By the end of 1933 Marshall had opened his own practice in Baltimore.

The office consisted of one small room that Marshall shared with his secretary. To save money, Buster Marshall decorated it with secondhand furniture, and Marshall's mother donated her own living room rug. Though his practice was run on a limited budget, Marshall was hopeful that he would soon be able to make a name for himself. He was eager to become a successful lawyer.

Why I Joined the NAACP

In the following passage, excerpted from Michael D. Davis and Hunter R. Clark's book on Thurgood Marshall, Marshall describes his view of the NAACP.

"[The cases fought for by the NAACP] served as guide posts in a sustained fight for full citizenship for Negroes. They have broadened the scope of protection guaranteed by the Thirteenth, Fourteenth and Fifteenth Amendments . . . in the fields of the right to register to vote, equal justice before the law, Negroes on juries, [and] segregation. . . . In addition, they broaden the interpretation of constitutional rights for all citizens and extend civil liberties for whites, as well as Negroes."

The timing of his new venture, however, could not have been worse. The United States was still suffering from the Great Depression. Many people were still out of work or working at low-paying jobs. Most African Americans who lived in Marshall's area were lower middle class and had few extra dollars to spend on a lawyer. Paying clients were so few that Marshall, at the end of his first year in business, was nearly one thousand dollars in debt. Remembering those lean days, he said, "one day I'd bring two lunches, and the next day my secretary would bring two lunches, and sometimes we'd be the only two people in that office for weeks at a time."[17]

A client's inability to pay never stopped Marshall from taking a case, though. He was sympathetic to the people who came by his office. Most of his cases involved evicted tenants, wills, minor property cases, and various misdemeanors. But there were also people who came to Marshall who had clearly been unjustly treated by the law, and he would often take those cases for free even if he had to pass up other income-producing cases. Marshall's secretary used to say that he "had a genius for ignoring cases that might earn him money."[18]

The Freebie Lawyer

Word spread through Baltimore's African-American community that Marshall was someone who could be counted on for help, even by those who could not pay. Marshall's concern for others and his generous nature had earned him a reputation as a lawyer who took cases for free. Local judges referred to him as a freebie and

As a young lawyer, Marshall was sympathetic to those who needed but were unable to pay for legal help. He was especially interested in civil rights law and would often take up such cases for free.

sent him plenty of nonpaying clients. Some of the cases Marshall worked on were sent to him by his old friend Houston, who had left Howard Law School in 1934 to take a position as special counsel for the NAACP in New York. Houston began sending NAACP cases from the Baltimore area to Marshall, and by the end of his second year of practice, Marshall was becoming well versed in civil rights law.

Among his victories was a case in which Marshall represented African-American schoolteachers against the state of Maryland. The schoolteachers were demanding that they be paid the same wages as their white counterparts. When Marshall became involved, black teachers were being paid the same salary as the janitors. The yearly salary of African-American principals, for example, was only $612, while white principals were paid $1,475 a year. Marshall successfully argued the case, and the school board raised the salaries.

While Marshall found the variety of cases referred to him by the NAACP personally fulfilling, he knew that soon the NAACP would have to focus its legal efforts in one direction. The organization needed a long-range plan to attack segregation on a broad scale. The NAACP's effort, Executive Secretary Walter White said, would be a "large-scale, widespread, dramatic campaign to give the Southern Negro his constitutional rights, his political and civil equality . . . and to give the Negroes equal rights in the public schools."[19] NAACP leaders believed that the best hope for obtaining civil rights for African Americans lay with the courts.

Nathan Margold, a Harvard-educated white lawyer and member of the NAACP, put together a 218-page plan outlining the organization's strategy for ending segregation. It called for the dismantling of the legal basis for segregation, which was called the separate-but-equal doctrine.

The *Plessy* Decision

The separate-but-equal doctrine was based on an 1896 court case called *Plessy v. Ferguson*. The case involved the state of Louisiana and an African-American man named Homer Plessy. He was required to sit in the coloreds-only sections of restaurants, theaters, and public transportation. When Plessy tried to sit in the whites-only section of a train in Louisiana, he was brought to trial. Plessy's defense was that the Jim Crow segregation laws went against the Fourteenth Amendment, which gave all citizens "equal protection of the laws." The *Plessy* case went all the way to the Supreme Court.

Since the Supreme Court is the highest court in the land, its decisions are very important. The Court consists of nine judges called justices. When the justices rule on a particular case, that ruling will be used to decide future similar cases in the lower courts. The Court looks for cases that can be used to clarify an area of law. The lower courts can then use these Supreme Court cases to guide their decision making. *Plessy v. Ferguson* was such a case.

In the *Plessy* case the Supreme Court decided in favor of Ferguson, who was acting as an agent of the state of Louisiana. They ruled that Louisiana, or any state, could legally require separate seating on trains as long as the seating accommodations were equal. The majority opinion of the Court was that segregation laws were not unconstitutional if they were "enacted in good faith for the promotion of the public good, and not for the annoyance or oppression of a particular class."[20] The ruling gave the states the support they needed to enforce their current Jim Crow laws and to enact more of them. When any of these laws were challenged, the local courts relied on the *Plessy* decision as a precedent that segregation was indeed constitutional.

The *Plessy* decision had given states a legal way to continue discriminating against African Americans, but the NAACP was committed to obtaining civil rights for all Americans in spite of the decision. The Margold plan outlined an orderly step-by-step legal attack on the separate-but-equal doctrine using education-related cases as the foundation of the attack.

Houston and Marshall agreed that they should choose their cases carefully. They needed to select cases in which it would be clear that a student was denied admission to a school solely because of race. They also had to be able to show that the state could not offer the student an equal education at a separate facility.

Houston and Marshall found the case they were looking for in Donald Gaines Murray. He had applied to the law school at the University of Maryland and, like all previous African-American applicants, had been rejected. Marshall realized that this case had all of the elements he and Houston were looking for. Murray had been an honor student at Amherst College in Massachusetts, had no criminal background, and came from a solid, respectable family. Only his race made Murray different from the other applicants who had been accepted to the university's

When Donald Gaines Murray (middle) was turned down for admission to the University of Maryland because of his race, Marshall (left) and Houston (right) sued the university on his behalf. The case especially appealed to Marshall since this was the same school that had rejected Marshall years before.

A Letter of Appeal

After being denied admission to the University of Maryland Law School, Donald Murray appealed the decision to the University of Maryland board of regents in a letter drafted by Marshall on Murray's behalf. This excerpt is from Davis and Clark's biography of Marshall.

"I am a citizen of the State of Maryland and fully qualified to become a student at the University of Maryland Law School. No other State institution affords a legal education. The arbitrary action of the officials of the University of Maryland in returning my application was unjust and unreasonable and contrary to the Constitution and laws of the United States and the Constitution and laws of the State. I, therefore, appeal to you as the governing body of the University to accept the enclosed application and money order and to have my qualifications investigated within a reasonable time. I am ready, willing, and able to meet all requirements as a student, to pay whatever dues are required of residents of the State, and to apply myself diligently to my work."

law school. The case had one additional appeal for Thurgood Marshall. When he graduated from Howard University, he had said, "my first idea was to get even with Maryland for not letting me go to its law school."[21] Marshall had never forgotten the university's rejection of his own application. The thought of overturning the university's race policy—and embarrassing the regents in the process—gave Marshall motivation.

Getting Even

Marshall and Houston sued the University of Maryland on April 20, 1935, on behalf of Donald Murray. They asked the state court to order the university to admit Murray to the law school for the fall semester. The case went to court on June 18, 1935.

During questioning, university president Raymond A. Pearson conceded that his university's law school was the only accredited law school in the state and that the separate school for African Americans was only an unaccredited junior college.

In his closing argument, Marshall pointed out that while the university could offer Murray a separate education at the Princess Anne Academy, it could not provide an equal one. Marshall stated:

What's at stake here is more than the rights of my client; . . . it's the moral commitment stated in our country's creed. . . . Donald Murray was not sent to a separate school of the University of Maryland. . . . Donald Murray was excluded from the University of Maryland. [22]

Judge Eugene O'Dunne agreed. On June 25, 1935, he ordered that Donald Murray be admitted to the University of Maryland Law School.

It was a huge victory for Marshall, Houston, and the NAACP. NAACP official Juanita Jackson Mitchell described the effect the case had on African Americans by saying that it "set the colored people in Baltimore on fire. They were euphoric with victory. . . . We didn't know about the Constitution. He [Marshall] brought us the Constitution as a document like Moses brought the people the Ten Commandments." [23]

The state of Maryland appealed to the next higher court, the Maryland Court of Appeals. The following January the appeals court upheld Judge O'Dunne's ruling with a strong statement: "Compliance with the Constitution cannot be deferred at the will of the State. Whatever system it adopts for legal education now must furnish equality of treatment now." [24] The decision by the appeals court meant that the state of Maryland would have to comply with O'Dunne's ruling immediately.

Maryland accepted defeat. Marshall was thrilled. When a reporter suggested that the Murray case was "sweet revenge," Marshall agreed that it was "wonderful. I enjoyed it to no end." He explained that the university "wouldn't let [me] go to the law school because I was a Negro and all through law school I decided I'd make them pay for it, and so when I got out and passed the bar, I proceeded to make them pay for it." [25]

Marshall (far right) meets with members of the NAACP. Winning the discrimination suit against the University of Maryland was an important part of the NAACP's plan to end educational inequality.

Though Marshall and Houston were happy about winning the Murray case, they were also disappointed, because the decision affected only the state of Maryland. They had hoped that the university would appeal the case all the way to the U.S. Supreme Court. They wanted to take cases like Donald Murray's to the highest court in the land, because a Supreme Court ruling in their favor was a necessary part of the NAACP's plan to desegregate education nationwide.

A Valuable Team Member

After the victory in the Murray case, the NAACP executive board was convinced that they needed Marshall on their legal team full-time. In 1936 they offered him the position of assistant special counsel, working directly under his mentor and friend Charles Houston. Houston sent the job offer to Marshall after adding a personal note to help sway him. The note read "You have been more than faithful in giving of your time to the Association and I know this has meant a sacrifice of private practice, so you can be assured I will do everything in my power to try to make some provisions for you."[26]

The provisions were a two-hundred-dollar-a-month salary for six months but no guarantees past the first six months. Also, to be able to accept Houston's offer, Marshall would have to give up his private law practice in Baltimore and move to New York. Marshall joked that closing his office "would mean a loss of practically no profit," as he had been handling mainly NAACP cases for the past year to the detriment of his own practice. He wrote an enthusiastic acceptance letter to Walter White, head of the NAACP, saying that "I have an opportunity now to do what I have always dreamed of doing! That is, to actually concentrate on the type of work the Association is doing."[27]

3 On the Road for the NAACP

Thurgood Marshall and Charles Houston knew that the fight for social equality would be long and exhausting. The two men also knew they could never win the war for civil rights alone; they needed an army to help fight their battles. They needed a corps of dedicated attorneys who could challenge discrimination in courtrooms across the South. Their first step was to organize a network of attorneys who were willing to take on civil rights cases for free, because most of those bringing the lawsuits were too poor to pay. Houston and Marshall traveled through Virginia, Georgia, Alabama, Mississippi, and North and South Carolina visiting Howard Law School graduates and convincing them they had an obligation to take civil rights cases. Marshall and Houston reminded the young lawyers that they had become attorneys against staggering odds; now it was time to help those who would come after them.

Building an Army

In a memorandum to Howard University president Mordecai Johnson, Houston outlined the role he saw for Howard law graduates. The memorandum he wrote to Johnson contained the same message he had passed on earlier to his students. He wrote:

> Every group must justify and interpret itself in terms of the general welfare; the only justification for the Howard University school of law, in a city having seven white law schools, is that it is doing a distinct, necessary work for the social good, . . . the indispensable social function of eliminating legal racial discrimination in America. . . . The Negro lawyer must be trained as a social engineer and group interpreter due to the Negro's social and political condition. The Negro lawyer must be prepared to anticipate, guide and interpret his group's advancement.[28]

The army of lawyers Houston and Marshall recruited was the frontline in the battle for civil rights. These lawyers made their services available to the community for free and they filed the initial lawsuits. When one of these suits matched the NAACP's plan, the frontline lawyers would contact the organization and bring Houston and Marshall in on the case.

As they rushed from one case to the next, Houston and Marshall had what they jokingly referred to as an office on wheels. Their office was usually Marshall's car.

Marshall (center) stands with members of the NAACP legal team that he recruited to challenge discrimination cases in courtrooms across America.

"Charlie would sit in my car—I had a little old beat-up '29 Ford—and type out the briefs."[29]

Fighting for Educational Equality

Buoyed by the success of the *Murray* case, the NAACP board began looking for another suit they could use to bring an end to educational inequality. Marshall found it in the case of Lloyd L. Gaines, a twenty-five-year-old St. Louis student who had been denied admission to the University of Missouri Law School.

Marshall was excited about this case because the university had provided written evidence that Gaines was being denied admission solely because of his race. The University of Missouri board of curators, or regents, passed a resolution on March 27, 1936, that said the university had "in effect forbidden the attendance of . . . a colored student at the University of Missouri. . . . Therefore . . . the application of said Lloyd L. Gaines . . . is rejected."[30] When Marshall read the resolution, he knew that this was a perfect case for the NAACP.

When talking about the case later to biographer Carl Rowan, Marshall stated:

They gave us a legal gift that was bigger than anything we could expect at Christmas. The problem in all these education cases was that the bastards never wanted to fight on the real legal issues. They didn't want a challenge to state actions based solely on race, so they always tried some subterfuge [deception] of pretending that blacks were excluded because they had body odor or might put some VD [venereal disease] on the toilet seat. They wanted judges to believe that all blacks, however clean, intellectually brilliant, patriotic, or whatever were being kept out of the state university for practical reasons other than racial discrimination. . . .

I couldn't believe it when the curators made it clear in their instructions to the registrar that Gaines was being rejected solely because of his race. Hell, the curators saved the NAACP about a hundred thousand dollars, which it didn't have, by that admission.[31]

On April 15, 1936, Marshall filed *Lloyd L. Gaines v. S.W. Canada, Registrar, U. of Mo.*, a suit that stated that by excluding "a qualified Negro citizen and resident of the state from the school of law of the University of Missouri, which is maintained by tax money which Negroes help to pay, solely on account of his color,"[32] the university had violated the Fourteenth Amendment.

In 1936 Marshall sued the University of Missouri Law School on behalf of Lloyd L. Gaines (pictured). Since the University of Missouri openly admitted that Gaines had been rejected solely because of his race, Marshall saw this case as the perfect opportunity to change the law that allowed racial discrimination at educational institutions.

With the curators' resolution on file, Marshall thought the case would be quickly won. But what Marshall thought would be an easy victory for the NAACP turned into a prolonged legal battle. One of the reasons the case lasted more than

Be It Resolved

On March 27, 1936, the University of Missouri board of curators passed a resolution to keep African-American student Lloyd L. Gaines out of the law school. The following excerpt is from Carl T. Rowan's Dream Makers, Dream Breakers: The World of Justice Thurgood Marshall.

"Whereas, Lloyd L. Gaines, colored, has applied for admission to the School of Law of the University of Missouri, and

Whereas, the people of Missouri, both in the Constitution and in the Statutes of the State, have provided for the separate education of white students and negro students, and have thereby in effect forbidden the attendance of a white student at Lincoln University, or a colored student at the University of Missouri, and

Whereas, the Legislature of the State of Missouri, in response to the demands of the citizens of Missouri has established at Jefferson City, Missouri, for Negroes, a modern and efficient school known as Lincoln University, and has invested the Board of Curators of that institution with full power and authority to establish such departments as may be necessary to offer students of that institution opportunities equal to those offered at the University, and have further provided, pending the full development of Lincoln University, for the payment, out of the public treasury, of the tuition, at universities in adjacent states, of colored students desiring to take any course of study not being taught at Lincoln University, and

Whereas, it is the opinion of the Board of Curators that any change in the State system of separate instruction which has been heretofore established, would react to the detriment of both Lincoln University and the University of Missouri,

Therefore, Be It Resolved, that the application of said Lloyd L. Gaines be and it hereby is rejected and denied, and that the Registrar and the Committee on Entrance be instructed accordingly."

two and a half years was that Marshall had a tough time at first proving that the separate education offered to Gaines was inferior to the one he would receive at the University of Missouri. During the first hearing none of the university or state officials would testify that students attending the University of Missouri Law School received a better education in Missouri law than students attending an out-of-state school. Furthermore, the defendants argued that Missouri had been a leader among segregated states in providing education for African Americans by opening the all-black Lincoln University in Jefferson City, Missouri, in 1866. One of the assumptions the court held was that if the state were to add a law school at Lincoln, it would be a quality school and provide students with a good education. As the hearing progressed, Marshall and Houston's confidence waned. Houston wrote to his staff: "It is beyond expectation that the court will decide in our favor, so we had just as well get ready for the appeal."[33] The university won the first round when the local court ruled in its favor on July 27, 1936. Undeterred, Marshall appealed the lower court's decision. His appeal was ruled against at the circuit court level and again at the Missouri Supreme Court.

Marshall took the *Gaines* case all the way to the U.S. Supreme Court, which ruled in Gaines's favor on December 12, 1938. The Court stated that

> as an individual [Gaines] was entitled to the equal protection of the laws, and the State was bound to furnish him within its border facilities for legal education substantially equal to those which the State there afforded for persons of the white race,

Case by case, Marshall worked tirelessly to ensure educational equality for all Americans.

whether or not other negroes sought the same opportunity. . . . The judgement of the Supreme Court of Missouri is reversed.[34]

Marshall was elated. After years of frustrating work, he had won admission for Gaines and taken another step toward ending segregated education. As part of its opinion, the Supreme Court wrote that a state had the "duty when it provides . . . training to furnish it to the resident of the State upon the basis of . . . equality."[35] Unlike the *Murray* case, which applied only to Maryland, the *Gaines* case could be used as a precedent to provide educational equality nationwide.

But Marshall's victory was short-lived, and he never had the satisfaction of seeing

Marshall stands next to one of his clients while she meets with the dean of admissions at the University of Oklahoma Law School. Though she was not admitted to the law school, the university later announced it was establishing a separate law school for black students to comply with an order by the U.S. Supreme Court to provide equal facilities. Marshall would argue again that separate was not equal.

Gaines attend law school: Gaines had disappeared. Marshall, the NAACP, Gaines's family, and various newspapers tried to locate him, but with no success. There were rumors that Gaines had tired of the fight and was working under a series of assumed names in other states to avoid publicity. There also were darker rumors that the student had been killed or had been threatened with physical violence and was hiding in fear. None of these rumors was confirmed, but Gaines was not heard from again.

Since the student had disappeared, Gaines's application for law school had to be dismissed. Marshall remembered the case as a bittersweet victory. "I remember *Gaines* as one of our greatest victories, but I have never lost the pain of having so many people spend so much time and money on him, only to have him disappear,"[36] Marshall later said.

Even though the application was dismissed, the publicity it garnered helped build public support for equal education for African Americans. *Time* magazine, the *New York Times*, and the *New York Herald Tribune* all carried stories in support of Marshall and the NAACP. The *Gaines* case also gave the NAACP the legal groundwork it needed to fight educational discrimination in other states. Marshall said:

> This case produced the victory, the legal precedent, that we used to wipe out . . . [laws that allowed unequal education for African Americans] in Oklahoma, Texas, Louisiana, and other states. In *Gaines* we dragged the federal courts one more step away from [the doctrine of] "separate but equal."[37]

Chief Legal Counsel

After the *Gaines* case, Marshall and Houston kept a grueling schedule that left both men exhausted. Houston had been battling poor health for years, and the frantic pace he kept during this period finally took its toll. As the pressure of his work increased, Houston's chronic tuberculosis was compounded by cardiac problems, and his doctors warned him that he needed to slow down or he would die. In 1938 Houston decided to resign his position as chief legal counsel to the NAACP, and thirty-year-old Marshall stepped in to fill his place.

Describing his feelings about Houston's retirement, Marshall said,

> The first thing I thought about was not what it meant to me, but what a loss it was to the NAACP. No organization can afford to lose a dedicated legal giant like Charlie. Then I thought about why Houston was leaving. The man had ignored tuberculosis to give his life to the cause of freedom for Afro-Americans. I looked at his travel schedule from one end of America to the other and saw that it was a killer.[38]

Marshall carried on in the same manner as before but without Houston by his side. Without his mentor's help, Marshall's schedule was even busier than before. As his reputation spread and his name became synonymous with civil rights, his job became more tense and more dangerous. Tension was building in the South, and threats against black litigants and black lawyers frequently turned to violence; Marshall was often threatened. He later told the story of stopping in one Mississippi town where he was confronted by a white man carrying a gun. Marshall related: "He said, 'Nigger boy, what are you doing here?' And I said, 'Well, I'm waiting for the train to Shreve-

port.' And he said, 'There's only one more train that comes through here, and that's the four o'clock, and you'd better be on it because the sun is never going down on a live nigger in this town.'"[39] When commuting among courthouses, Marshall often traveled with an armed escort, and during his stay in unfriendly towns, he frequently moved from house to house to avoid becoming an easy target.

The Fund

But even the threat of violence did not deter Marshall; he vowed to expand the NAACP's fight. In October 1939 the NAACP Legal Defense and Educational Fund (commonly referred to as the Fund) was established, and Marshall was named its director-counsel. The Fund's charter stated that it was established

> to render free legal aid to Negroes who suffer legal injustice because of their race or color and cannot afford to employ legal assistance. To seek and promote educational opportunities denied to Negroes because of their color. To conduct research and publish information on educational facilities and inequalities furnished for Negroes out of public funds and on the status of the Negro in American life.[40]

Marshall described how the Fund functioned in its early days:

> We [would] get either a letter or a telephone call or telegram from either a person or a lawyer saying that they have got a problem involving discrimination on the part of race or color and

it [appeared] to be a legal problem. Then the question [was] . . . whether or not we [would] help. If it [was] a worthwhile problem, we [looked] into it. . . . If the investigation conducted either from the New York office or through one of our local lawyers [revealed] that there [was] discrimination because of race or color and legal assistance [was] needed, we [furnished] that legal assistance in the form of either helping in payment of the costs or helping in the payment of lawyer's fees, and mostly [in] legal research in the preparation of briefs and materials.[41]

With the assistance of the Fund, the NAACP was able to expand its fight for social justice. During this time Marshall found himself working on a wide variety of lawsuits dealing with civil rights, and his fight for social justice was winning him national attention. Marshall was soon dubbed with the nickname Mr. Civil Rights. His reputation was summed up by the trustees of Howard University when they awarded Marshall a citation of recognition which read, in part:

> You have fully justified the exceptional promise of your student days. . . . You are winning significant and enduring victories for a disadvantaged people. Your unceasing labors are opening the way for the achievement of an even greater measure of justice and equality under the law. Your star still rises, and though it is not yet at its zenith the brilliance of your accomplishment and the value of your service to your fellow man [has] already marked you as an advocate, a legal scholar and humanitarian of the first magnitude.[42]

Amid the praise, Marshall never lost sight of his goal. He would be satisfied only when all citizens were guaranteed their equal rights under the law. Marshall's feelings were summed up in his testimony to the Judiciary Committee of the U.S. Senate when he said, "Segregation has to go the way chattel slavery went, and go soon."[43] Marshall believed that segregation would not end until African Americans had the ability to vote and select their leaders, thus gaining a full voice in government.

Blind Justice

The Fourteenth Amendment guarantees equal rights under the law, but too often African Americans have found that justice was not color-blind. The inequality that African Americans faced in many police stations and courts was summed up for Marshall in the 1941 W. D. Lyons case in Hugo, Oklahoma. Lyons was a black man who had been accused of murdering a white couple and their four-year-old son.

After eleven days in an Oklahoma jail, Lyons signed a statement confessing to the murders. Before signing the statement, Lyons had not been allowed to talk to a lawyer, and there were rumors that his confession had come after hours of beatings at the hands of local police. Only after signing the confession was Lyons finally allowed to see a lawyer. Stanley Belden, the white lawyer who took Lyons's case, quickly called on the NAACP and Marshall for help.

In his letter, Belden wrote:

> I don't think they have a shred of evidence that doesn't depend on the con-

fession, and if you could hear the full details of the torture which produced the . . . confession. . . . No jury could believe it was voluntary. . . . It will be nip and tuck whether [the jury will] believe the police [and] the confession, or Lyons.[44]

When Marshall took the case, he knew he was taking his life in his hands. Most of the white citizens in Hugo were convinced of Lyons's guilt and they resented an outsider, with a reputation of winning the cases he tried, coming to Lyons's aid. When he arrived in Hugo, Oklahoma, Marshall found that a group of African Americans from the town had banded together to protect him. They had smuggled weapons from out of state and appointed themselves his armed bodyguards. Marshall received numerous death threats while he was investigating the case, and he

had to travel to and from the courthouse with armed bodyguards each day.

After examining the evidence and reading Lyons's pretrial statements, Marshall was convinced that Lyons was innocent. Marshall questioned the police on the witness stand, and had them describe how they had tortured Lyons to win his confession. One witness described how ten different men had taken turns beating Lyons until he finally confessed. Marshall's arguments were so convincing that public opinion about the case slowly began to change. Even C. A. Colclasure, the father of the murdered woman, felt that Lyons was innocent and that the confession was a sham. Colclasure testified that the police had told him that they had beaten Lyons until he would sign a confession.

But even Colclasure's testimony was not enough to sway the all-white jury.

Segregation Is Discrimination

In an article that he wrote for the New York Age *in December 1945 Marshall expressed his feelings about segregation. The following excerpt from that article is quoted in Carl T. Rowan's* Dream Makers, Dream Breakers.

"On the question of whether or not it is lawful to segregate American citizens solely because of their race or color, most of the courts in the land, including the United States Supreme Court, have unfortunately adopted the fiction of 'separate but equal.' Under this fiction there has grown up a group of court decisions holding that the equality guaranteed by the Fourteenth Amendment can be given in a segregated system providing equal facilities are maintained. This fiction built up by the courts must at some time be cast aside in favor of the establishment of a policy that segregation is discrimination."

On Thursday, January 30, 1941, the jury found Lyons guilty of murder and sentenced him to life in prison. Lyons was sent to McAlester prison, where he remained until he was pardoned by the Oklahoma governor in 1965. The verdict was a bitter defeat for Marshall. This case proved to Marshall beyond a doubt that the American system was biased against African Americans.

The Time Has Come

In 1944 Marshall summed up his feelings about racial discrimination in a speech to eight hundred delegates at the NAACP's convention in Chicago. In his speech, Marshall told the convention:

> We must not be delayed by people who say "the time is not ripe," nor should we proceed with caution for fear of destroying the status quo. Persons who deny to us our civil rights should be brought to justice now. Many people believe the time is always "ripe" to discriminate against Negroes. All right then—the time is always "ripe" to bring them to justice.[45]

For Marshall the time was ripe, and he was determined to do his part to fight social inequality.

4 Taking On the Military

In 1941 America entered World War II, and African Americans wanted to join the military and help defend their country. But instead of fighting for their country, most black soldiers found themselves tied to menial jobs and facing discrimination both at their posts and away from them. Marshall said of the era:

> When war came, blacks wanted to fight for America, in the skies, on the seas, on the battlegrounds of European towns and African deserts. But . . . colored Americans could only serve in Jim Crow units that did the menial chores of cooking, cleaning up, loading dangerous ammunition. . . . It was just one utterly stupid manifestation of the grip of racism on this society.[46]

And according to historian John Egerton, "segregation dogged all African Americans in uniform, wherever they went in the war years—within the ranks of their units, in recreation halls and social clubs, on furlough in the towns around their bases."[47]

The Ninety-third Infantry Division, the first all-black division to be formed during World War II, awaits an attack command during drills. Though some blacks did engage in combat, most were relegated to menial chores, such as cleaning and ditch digging.

Ironically, white prisoners of war had more rights than the African-American soldiers who guarded them. German prisoners were allowed to eat in the dining cars of the trains and hotels they were held in, but their black guards either had to eat at separate tables or not eat at all.

Thirty-three-year-old Marshall was not drafted during the war. Marshall later said of the war years:

I think the people on my draft board agreed secretly that they didn't need a damned trouble making lawyer in the military. But every day I knew that I was in the army, in heart and spirit, when I got an endless string of telephone calls, telegrams, letters, from colored GIs, or their wives, partners, girlfriends . . . heart-wrenching stories of bigotry. . . . Nobody was into that war more than I was.[48]

Desks at the NAACP were covered with letters from soldiers and their families complaining about discrimination within the military, and the conditions he read about in the letters were intolerable to Marshall. "War is hell in every place and time," Marshall said, "but it was a special hell for people who were forced to fight for freedoms they had never known, for liberties that thousands of them would die without knowing."[49]

At Marshall's urging the NAACP quickly joined the fight for the black soldiers' rights. One of the first military cases Marshall became involved in was that of a Howard University student named Yancey Williams. During the early 1940s the U.S. Army was recruiting thirty thousand pilots a year to be part of a new branch of the armed forces called the Army Air Corps. Williams, who already had a pilot's license, volunteered for the service, but was rejected from the pilot program because he was an African American. The NAACP took the case, and Marshall won for Williams the right to fly for the Army Air

We Aren't Going to Take It Anymore

In Voices of Freedom *James Hicks, a black officer during World War II, writes about blacks' change in attitude following the war.*

"I think that when black veterans of World War II returned home, they were really an influence on their communities. They were activists and they had been trained, and of course when they said, 'No more of this Jim Crow' or what have you, the people, that is the black people, picked it up.

I think there was extreme resentment among the black veterans when they came back, because they felt, 'I paid my dues over there and I'm not going to take this anymore over here.'"

Because of the efforts of Marshall and the NAACP, the army agreed to form an all-black group of pilots during World War II. The successful Ninety-ninth Pursuit Squadron (pictured) broadened the role that blacks were allowed in the military.

Corps. Marshall's work opened the door for African-American soldiers to become officers and full participants in the armed forces.

Marshall was elated, but he knew it was only a partial victory. The army agreed, as a test, to train thirty-three black pilots to become the Ninety-ninth Pursuit Squadron, which would be an all-African-American squadron. A special training school was set up at the Tuskegee Institute, a black college in Alabama, to train the pilots. Throughout the program the pilots had to fight for the right to continue their train-ing and then, upon graduation, the right to be allowed to go to Europe and join the war. Eventually the pilots won their battle and the Ninety-ninth went to Europe. The squadron proved so successful that the army commissioned another all-black squadron. This was a victory for African Americans, but a small one. Even though blacks could now become pilots, enlistment in flying squadrons was open to a very small percentage of the African-American volunteers.

For the majority of African Americans who entered the armed services during the war, the most they could hope for was a menial job as a ditch digger, food attendant, or latrine cleaner. And even for the pilots the armed service they had fought so hard to be a part of was strictly segregated. Black soldiers were forced to travel on separate buses, eat in separate dining areas, and attend segregated theaters on base.

The Nation Reacts

Marshall's work on behalf of black soldiers and the demands from the African-American community caught the public's attention and finally brought the plight of the African-American citizen to the White House. In 1946, President Harry Truman established the President's Commission on Civil Rights to investigate how the government could help end segregation in the United States. The commission's task was "to determine whether and in what respect . . . the authority and means possessed by the federal, state and local governments may be strengthened and improved to safeguard the civil rights of the people."[50]

The commission's findings echoed Marshall's belief that separate could never be equal. Its 178-page report, titled *To Secure These Rights*, painted a bleak picture of the state of civil rights in America. The report stated that the policy of separate but equal was a failure and that the belief that equality exists in a segregated society "is one of the outstanding myths of American history." The commission's recommendation was to "cure the disease as well as treat its symptoms [by] the elimination of segregation, based on race, color, creed, or national origin, from American life."[51]

President Truman helped advance social equality by signing a 1948 order ending segregation in the military.

In June 1947 Truman spoke at the NAACP's thirty-eighth annual convention, the first U.S. president ever to do so. He said, "We must make the federal government a friendly, vigilant defender of the rights and equalities of all Americans. And again, I mean all Americans."[52]

Truman stressed that the United States must change and change immediately: "We cannot wait another decade or another generation to remedy these evils [insult, intimidation, violence, prejudice, and intolerance]. We must work, as never before, to cure them now."[53] To prove his commitment to social equality, in 1948 Truman issued Executive Order 9981 ending segregation in the U.S. armed forces.

But even the president's order did not end discrimination. Many military commanders were reluctant to integrate troops and segregation and discrimination continued.

The Korean Conflict

When the Korean conflict began in June 1950, Marshall found himself dealing with many of the same issues he had fought throughout World War II. Officially segregation and discrimination had ended, but in reality life was much the same for soldiers in Korea as it had been for their predecessors. While African Americans were being used as frontline soldiers and were publicly praised and awarded medals and commendations, in private they were still treated as unequal and inferior. The NAACP received letters from black enlisted men complaining about the treatment they received from their commanding officers. The letters complained about the high rate of courts-martial of African-American troops and that black soldiers were being convicted unfairly and without the benefit of a proper trial.

Looking at the reports, Marshall found that most of the soldiers were being court-martialed for violating the Seventy-fifth Article of War regarding misbehavior in front of the enemy, or cowardice. This article could be used to try a soldier on a wide range of activities and gave the courts great latitude in doling out punishment.

Marshall decided to personally investigate the courts-martial of thirty-six African Americans from the Third Battalion who

General MacArthur reviews troops during the Korean War. Though segregation and discrimination were illegal at the time, African Americans were still not treated with equality.

had appealed to the NAACP for assistance. The Third Battalion was an all-African-American unit that had won international praise for retaking the Korean city of Yechon on July 28, 1950, after a bloody sixteen-hour battle. The same men who had been commended by the military for their bravery at the battle of Yechon were now being tried for cowardice during later engagements. "It seemed hard to believe that these men could change over from heroes to cowards, all within a few days, even under the violent pressures of warfare,"[54] Marshall said of the appeals.

Marshall's first action was to fly to Asia and visit each of the imprisoned men and hear his version of the charges.

I spent three weeks making daily trips to the stockade in which they were confined—just outside of Tokyo—and

interviewed thirty-four of the thirty-six accused men who had written for our assistance prior to my leaving New York. The other two were hospitalized at the time. I also talked to many others who requested assistance while I was there.[55]

In addition to meeting with the prisoners in Japan, Marshall interviewed witnesses who belonged to the same units as the accused men. During his stay in Asia, Marshall interviewed more than eighty people. From Japan Marshall flew to Korea to visit frontline troops and discover how they were being treated by their commanders. During his investigation, Marshall found a pattern of false charges and hurried trials, some lasting less than fifteen minutes. In one case he found a black soldier charged with "misbehavior in front of the enemy" who had been

Bravery Under Fire

The following excerpt from Michael Davis and Hunter Clark's book on Thurgood Marshall is a memorandum written on September 11, 1950, by Lieutenant Colonel J. T. Corley when he took command of the 24th Infantry Regimental.

"Upon assumption of command, I cannot help but express my opinion of the Fighting 24th United States Infantry. In the sixty days of continuous combat, you have withstood a 'toughness of battle' which I have not seen in five campaigns in Africa, Sicily and Europe with the First Infantry Division. You have held ground against superior forces. You have lived up to the regimental motto 'Semper Paratus' [Always Prepared]. The first United States victory in Korea was your action at Yech'on. It has been noted in Congress. The people back home cover in detail your efforts on 'Battle Hill' west of Haman, Korea. Other units have been unable to accomplish what depleted companies of the Fighting 24th have done."

A soldier rests after injuring his leg while fighting on the front line. While African-American soldiers were publicly commended for their bravery, privately, many were discriminated against.

sentenced to ten years at hard labor, even though the soldier was able to prove that he had been in an army hospital during the period that the charges accused him of dereliction.

Marshall also found that sentences for African-American soldiers were much more severe than those for white soldiers: Thirty-two black soldiers had been convicted under the Seventy-fifth Article of War from August through October 1950, and their sentences ranged from ten years at hard labor to death. During the same period only two white soldiers were convicted under the same article; one was drunk while on duty and deserted his post, and the other was a sentry who fell asleep on duty. The first soldier was given a five-year sentence, which was later reduced to one year, and the second soldier was acquitted. Of his findings Marshall said, "justice in Korea may have been blind, but not color-blind."[56]

Marshall reported to the NAACP board in 1951 that

> the pattern is little varied from war to war. First come reports from the front of some heroic deed done by Negro soldiers, an achievement to indicate the courage with which these men are facing the enemy and their ability to take the toughest kind of fighting. And then suddenly the reports change as if in a concerted effort to discredit the record of Negro fighting men. The

tales we are beginning to hear are of incompetency, failure and cowardice—accounts which would make it appear that Negroes are not capable of combat duty and should be restricted to labor battalions. [57]

The cowardice charges were based on such incidents as a soldier failing to keep up with his comrades during a march and another soldier who was not at his post in a war zone. In the first case Marshall discovered that the soldier was marching while suffering from a sprained ankle and that the soldier missing from his post was actually on sick leave in a military hospital. Marshall proved in case after case that the charges of cowardice were based on inaccuracies.

The discrimination faced by African-American soldiers was unacceptable, Marshall said.

As long as we have racial segregation in the army, we will have the type of injustice of which these courts-martial are typical. Men who are daily exposing themselves to injury and death at the hands of the enemy should not be subjected to injustice, additional hardships, and unnecessary danger solely because of race. [58]

Following Marshall's investigation, the army reduced sentences for twenty of the

---

Records Stacked to the Ceiling

During World War II and the Korean War, membership in the NAACP swelled, according to Constance Baker Motley, who was an NAACP Legal Defense and Educational Fund attorney during the 1940s. The following is taken from Henry Hampton and Steve Fayer's Voices of Freedom.

"The NAACP's membership almost doubled during that period [of World War II] from membership applications from black servicemen who recognized that the NAACP was the only organization they could turn to for assistance with what they believed to be a very pressing problem for them. And that is that they received disproportionately harsher sentences than white servicemen for any crime which they committed. They felt this was a tremendous grievance that something had to be done about. When I first went to work at the NAACP Legal Defense and Educational Fund, in the summer of 1944, we had court-martial records stacked to the ceiling that had to be reviewed and appeals taken to military review boards in Washington, [D.C.,] so our legal efforts were concentrated in the area of trying to get these servicemen's sentences reduced, if not the conviction reversed."

Black soldiers move up to the firing line in Korea. After visiting Korea, Marshall found the discrimination against black soldiers unacceptable and fought for the enforcement of Truman's Executive Order.

cases he had reviewed. NAACP executive secretary Walter White said that Marshall's trip "underscores the need for immediate elimination of segregation from the United States Army and for the full implementation of the President's [Truman's] Executive Order."[59]

Clarence Mitchell, of the NAACP Washington bureau, echoed White's feelings when he testified before the Preparedness Subcommittee of the Senate Armed Services Committee in 1951. Mitchell said:

It is a frightful thing to contemplate that their government will call upon [blacks] to risk their lives in war and at the same time fail to protect them against undemocratic practices. . . . If the government has the power to draft a man, it also has the power to protect him wherever he may be stationed.[60]

Slowly, through the work of Marshall and the NAACP, the armed services began to change, and President Truman's plan for equality was fully implemented over time. As the armed services began to change, Marshall was able to turn his attention back to other areas of social inequality.

Chapter

5 The Beginning of the End

Even while he was fighting for the rights of U.S. military men overseas, Marshall never quit fighting to win equal educational opportunities for African-American students. When Marshall first joined the NAACP in the 1930s, the group had tried to prove that the separate educational facilities offered to African Americans were simply not equal to those offered to white students. Now Marshall began taking the cases even further. He no longer was content to prove that separate facilities were unequal. He started using court cases to prove that the basic idea of segregation was flawed and that the practice was psychologically damaging to both black and white students.

Texas Law

Marshall used his new tactics in the case of Herman Sweatt, a Texas postal worker who was denied admission to the University of Texas Law School due to his color. Following the denial, a state judge ordered Texas to establish a law school for Sweatt at Prairie View University in Houston, a vocational college for blacks.

Instead of trying to prove that the Prairie View facility would be unequal to the University of Texas Law School, Mar-

shall decided that it was time to challenge the sociological basis for segregation. During the trial, Marshall called on Robert Redfield, chairman of the anthropology department at the University of Chicago, to prove his point. Redfield, who held doctorates in both anthropology and law, dismissed the idea that blacks were inferior to whites intellectually. He also testified that segregation intensified distrust between races and inhibited the learning process for blacks. Marshall subsequently told the court, "There is no understandable factual basis for classification by race. . . . It is flat in the teeth of [directly opposed to] the Fourteenth Amendment."[61]

Marshall's arguments did not sway the judge. The Texas state court ruled against Sweatt, which gave Marshall the opportunity he had been waiting for. He appealed the state's decision to the U.S. Supreme Court, but it would be three years before the case reached the Supreme Court docket.

McLaurin v. Oklahoma State Regents

In the meantime Marshall continued using his new strategy in other cases. One of the most visible of these was the University of Oklahoma's rejection of George W. McLaurin's admission into the doctoral program in education. In 1948 Marshall took the case to the U.S. district court, which ordered Oklahoma to admit McLaurin.

The university complied with the letter, but not the spirit, of the law. McLaurin was admitted to the program but was kept completely segregated from his classmates. He was allowed in the same classroom, but he had to sit in an empty row separated from other students by a railing. McLaurin was allowed to eat in the cafeteria, but only during hours when white students were not present. Marshall challenged McLaurin's treatment by going back to the district court and claiming that McLaurin was being forced to suffer a "badge of inferiority" by the university's actions. Even McLaurin's classmates were outraged at the treatment he was being

forced to suffer. The district court ruled in the university's favor, and Marshall again appealed to the U.S. Supreme Court. Marshall hoped to use McLaurin's case to end the practice of separate but equal. McLaurin was being offered equal access to the same facilities as white students, but his separation from them ensured him an unequal education.

The cases of *Sweatt* and *McLaurin* came before the U.S. Supreme Court at the same time. The Court heard oral arguments in *Sweatt* and *McLaurin* over two days—April 3 and 4, 1950—and decided both cases on June 5, 1950. Marshall's team confronted the issue of the separate-but-equal doctrine head-on in both cases and tried to prove that there were no constitutional grounds for segregation. Lawyers for Oklahoma and Texas argued that the wording of the Fourteenth Amendment allowed for segregation.

The Best Law School

As excerpted from Randall Bland's book Private Pressure on Public Law, *Marshall argued in the* Sweatt *case that the University of Texas was denying a black student access to the best education possible.*

"If an enlightened citizenry is a necessary factor in the equation of democracy, then it follows that education is an integral part of the democratic process. Assuming that education is merely a privilege, it is one of such a particular and precious nature that those entrusted with its administration have a compelling duty rather than mere discretionary power to see that no distinctions are made on the basis of race, creed or color. Unless Texas has some purpose other than those democratic objectives . . . it must permit all persons without regard to class or race to participate in these benefits on an equal basis."

Marshall had hoped the Court would use the two cases to rule that segregation was illegal, but the Court did not examine the legality of segregation. In *Sweatt* the Court for the first time ordered an African American admitted to an all-white school because the black counterpart school provided by the state was not equal to it. In the Court's ruling, sending Sweatt to the lesser law school would deny him his constitutional right to "legal education equivalent to that offered by the State to students of other races."[62]

In *McLaurin* the Court held that the segregation of McLaurin within the University of Oklahoma handicapped his ability to learn. The Court said that "such restrictions impair and inhibit his ability to study, to engage in discussions and exchange views with other students, and, in general, to learn his profession."[63] The Court's ruling meant that McLaurin must be allowed to participate fully in all classes and university activities and must not be segregated from his peers.

The message of the *McLaurin* case was that an African-American student who had obtained admission to a university must be treated by the university the same as any other student. While the Court sidestepped the issue of the separate-but-equal doctrine, the decisions did state firmly that what was separate must be equal.

With the victory in the *McLaurin* and *Sweatt* cases, Marshall was ready for the biggest battle of his career: putting an end to the separate-but-equal doctrine by proving that separate could never be equal.

Striking Down Discrimination

A group led by James M. Nabrit, a law professor at Howard University, had been

James M. Nabrit (right) urged Marshall to challenge the constitutionality of segregation. Marshall agreed that this bold step needed to be taken to ensure equal rights for all Americans.

urging Marshall to turn the NAACP's focus to proving the whole idea of segregation was unconstitutional. They felt that to continue to fight for separate-but-equal facilities would cost African Americans more rights in the long term, because as long as black students were segregated, they would never truly be treated as equal. However, there were some leaders in the NAACP who felt this bold approach was too risky. They were afraid that if they attacked the separate-but-equal doctrine directly and took their case to the Supreme Court, they risked having the Court rule that segregation was constitutional. In response, Nabrit argued that the Court would be forced to rule segregation unconstitutional or else it would have to "take the blame if it dares to say to the entire world, 'Yes, democracy rests on a legalized caste system; segregation of races is legal.'"[64]

Marshall agreed with Nabrit, and following the *Sweatt* and *McLaurin* cases, Marshall decided to attack the whole doctrine of separate but equal.

Even as he made his decision, Marshall realized what a momentous task he faced. He would have to challenge the Supreme Court's earlier ruling in *Plessy v. Ferguson* and get it overruled. But Marshall felt that it was the only way to permanently ensure equal treatment for African Americans. To overturn the *Plessy* decision, Marshall knew he needed a new case that would expose the inequality of the separate but equal doctrine. He found the perfect case in South Carolina, where Harry Briggs was fighting for equal education for his children. Marshall stated "No state offers clearer proof than South Carolina that

separate school facilities and opportunities never have been, are not now, and never will be equal."[65]

Briggs v. Elliot

In 1951, Marshall came before a South Carolina district court with a case called *Briggs v. Elliot*. Briggs was suing the state of South Carolina over the inferior conditions of the blacks-only school his children attended in Clarendon County. Representing the state was R. W. Elliott, the chairman of the board of public schools in South Carolina's district 22 where the Briggs children attended school. Marshall knew that winning the case would be difficult. Only one of the three judges on the panel, Judge J. Waties Waring, looked favorably upon desegregation. The other two judges, John Parker and George Timmerman, wanted to maintain the status quo of separate-but-equal education.

In *Briggs v. Elliot* Marshall decided to concentrate on two key issues: the basic inequality of the segregated schools and the fact that segregation itself, even if the schools were equal, was harmful psychologically to the children involved.

The first issue in the *Briggs* case was clear-cut. It was easy for Marshall to show how much better the whites-only schools in the district were than the African-American schools. The whites-only schools had a greater variety and number of courses and the rooms were larger, cleaner, and better equipped. The whites-only schools also had fewer students per teacher than at the African-American schools. In the district there were three

schools for African Americans with 12 teachers and 808 students while the same district had two all-white schools staffed with 12 teachers for only 276 students. The differences were so easily demonstrated that South Carolina attorney general T. C. Callison did not even argue with Marshall. He agreed with each of Marshall's points but insisted that the differences in the schools were from lack of money, not from discrimination. Callison's defense to Marshall's argument about the physical condition of the blacks-only schools was to emphasize the state's intentions to improve the schools. Shortly before the case began, the South Carolina state assembly approved funding to upgrade the African-American schools to the level of the schools for whites. Callison argued that since the state had already approved the money to make the

Two Georgia classrooms contrast the conditions of segregated schools during the 1940s. African-American students endured overcrowded classrooms and inferior facilities, while white students enjoyed larger, less-crowded classrooms and more teachers.

Though many African Americans expressed their feelings that progress toward desegregation should be made slowly, NAACP executive secretary Walter White issued the following statement, taken from Carl T. Rowan's Dream Makers, Dream Breakers, *to explain the NAACP's position.*

"What have we to lose? Nothing! The law says conclusively that Negroes are entitled to equal facilities. And it appears that the standards of equality which the courts will apply will be more rigid than ever. If the Association now refrains from its attack on segregation per se, basing its cases on the right to equal facilities, all we can reasonably expect are decisions applying the *Plessy v. Ferguson* formula with stricter emphasis on the equality aspect of the separate-but-equal doctrine.

Since this is the worst we can expect in a court decision, regardless of the legal policy pursued, there is little logic in the contention that a frontal attack jeopardizes the Negro's fight for better educational opportunities. The stakes are high, but the hazards are relatively fewer than they were ten years ago."

schools equal, the court should not force the whites-only schools to allow African-American students.

Next, Marshall turned to the more complicated second issue—that of psychological damage—which would be the basis of his case. Marshall believed that to win the *Briggs* case he would have to prove that segregation caused stigmatic injury. (A stigma means being marked in some way that is shameful, degrading, or disgraceful.) Marshall hoped to show that when African-American children were segregated by the state, they were marked as inferior to the white children and that this stigma caused them to suffer an emotional and mental injury that would last all of their lives. Marshall told his team: "Our challenge is to convince Judge Parker and others on this panel, and eventually the Supreme Court, that stigmatic injury is real, it's cruel and it's forbidden by the Constitution."[66]

Clark and His Dolls

Marshall brought in New York psychologist Kenneth B. Clark to testify that it was psychologically harmful to separate white and black students, that segregation caused black students to think that they were bad or not as smart as the white children. In his research Clark had used dolls to help find out how the children saw themselves. During the test the black children labeled the dark-skinned dolls ugly and bad, the white-skinned dolls nice and pretty, yet the children also said the dark-skinned dolls were most like themselves physically and socially. Clark subsequently made a report on child psychology and segregation for the 1950 White House Midcentury Conference on Youth in which he stated that the African-American children had poor self-images. Clark believed that this was a direct result of segregation.

Marshall pointed out to the judges that "there were roadblocks built as a result of segregation in that county which made it impossible for those children to absorb education like the white children would normally do, and that it was a lasting injury, not a temporary one, but a lasting injury." He closed his arguments by stating simply:

The only dispute is as to what we mean by "equal." The mere fact that there are two equal physical buildings does not mean there is equality as intended by the Fourteenth Amendment. So we take the position that equality means all of the education that is offered by the state.[67]

In the Briggs *case Marshall tried to prove that separating white and black children marked black children as inferior and caused stigmatic injury.*

Even with Clark's testimony, Marshall lost the case. By a two-to-one vote the judges ruled in favor of South Carolina and segregation. Of the panel of three judges who heard the case, only Judge Waring disagreed with the decision. He issued a strongly worded dissent, stating:

Segregation is per se [in itself] inequality. As heretofore [previously] shown, the courts of this land have declared unequivocally [unquestionably] that segregation is not equality. But these decisions have pruned away only the noxious [harmful] fruits. Here in this case, we are asked to strike at its very root. . . . To me the situation is clear and important, particularly at this time when our national leaders are called upon to show to the world that our democracy means what it says.[68]

Even though Marshall hated any defeat, there were two positive points that came out of the loss in South Carolina. The *Briggs* case showed Marshall that even in the South, desegregation had support. And, by losing the *Briggs* case at the lower court level, Marshall could now take his fight to the U.S. Supreme Court.

The *Briggs* case was consolidated with four other cases that the NAACP had lost at lower court levels, and Marshall appealed the five cases to the Supreme Court in the summer of 1952. The Court slated the cases to be heard that December.

Chapter

6 Ending School Segregation

On December 9, 1952, Marshall presented his arguments to the U.S. Supreme Court in the most important case of his life: *Brown v. Board of Education*. He looked calm and confident as he walked into the courtroom, but he was not. "No matter how many times I argued there, I never got used to it. . . . Just the voice of the court crier [a court official who proclaims the orders of the Court] could make your knees shake."[69] Of the nine justices on the Court, the ones he was most worried about convincing that it was time to end segregation were Fred M. Vinson and Stanley F. Reed of Kentucky, and Tom C. Clark of Texas.

Each of the states that were involved in the five cases that made up *Brown v. Board*

Plaintiffs in one of the five cases that made up Brown v. Board of Education *assemble on the steps of Virginia's state capitol building. The cases were brought before the Supreme Court by parents who wanted to end segregation in public schools.*

Marshall speaks with John W. Davis, the eloquent South Carolina lawyer who opposed Marshall in the Brown *case.*

of Education sent a representative to present its side. The lawyers for Kansas, Delaware, District of Columbia, and Virginia were all well versed in arguments favoring segregation in education, but none was so eloquent and admired as the lawyer for South Carolina, John W. Davis. He combined an emotional style of speaking and a commanding presence. Davis argued passionately, pleading with the Court to let the people of the South make their own decisions about their children. Davis pointed out that in some counties, African-American children were the majority, not the minority. He said:

> If [desegregation] is done on the mathematical basis, with 30 children as a maximum . . . you would have 27 Negro children and 3 whites in one school room. Would that make the children any happier? Would they learn any more quickly? Would their lives be more serene? [70]

He cited the writings of co-founder of the NAACP W. E. B. Du Bois to support his stance that segregation was the "Southern way of life," desired by both whites and blacks.

In his closing arguments, Davis said:

> I have repeatedly seen wise and loving colored parents take infinite pains to force their little children into schools where the white children, white teachers, and white parents despised and resented the dark child, made a mock of it, neglected or bullied it, and literally rendered its life a living hell. Such parents want their children to "fight" this thing out—but . . . at what a cost! We shall get a finer, better balance, . . . [a] more capable and rounded personality by putting children in schools where they are wanted . . . than in thrusting them into hells where they are ridiculed and hated. [71]

He concluded by urging the justices to learn "the wishes of the parent, both white and colored, . . . before their children are forced into what may be an unwelcome contact." [72]

Davis and Marshall, along with J. Lee Rankin, assistant U.S. attorney, meet before giving their final arguments in Brown.

Even though Davis's speech angered Marshall, he kept his emotions to himself. He said, "I was so furious . . . that I just closed my eyes and told myself that I had to stick with our constitutional arguments."[73] In a calm and reasonable voice he began, using logic and the law to support his case. Marshall's response to Davis's argument: "While we are talking about the [feelings] of the people in South Carolina, I think we must . . . emphasize that [the] rights of minority people are not to be left to [the discretion] of the majority of the people."[74]

Marshall wanted to focus on each individual child's right to an education equal to the education that other children received. When Justice Felix Frankfurter asked him to define *equal*, Marshall said firmly "equal means getting the *same* thing, at the *same* time and in the *same* place."[75] He went on to say:

There is nothing involved in this case other than race and color. . . . If [United Nations official] Ralph Bunche were assigned to South Carolina, his children would have to go to a Jim Crow school. No matter how great anyone becomes, if he happens to have been born a Negro, regardless of his color, he is relegated to that school.[76]

Marshall knew that all of the justices had grave concerns about the effect of desegregation on the South. Though South Carolina's Davis had played up those concerns, saying that both the white and black children would suffer, Marshall took a different approach in his rebuttal. Marshall told the justices:

I got the feeling on hearing the points [Davis] made . . . that when you put a white child in a school with a lot of colored children, the child would fall apart. . . . Everybody knows that is not true. These same kids in Virginia and South Carolina . . . play in the streets together, they play on their farms together, they come out of school and play ball together. They have to be separated in school. . . . [Segregation] can't be [based solely on] color because there are Negroes as white as the drifted snow, with blue eyes, and they are just as segregated as the colored men. The only thing it can be is an inherent determination that the people who were formerly in slavery, regardless of anything else, shall be kept as near that stage as possible, and now is the time, we submit, that this court should make it clear that is not what our Constitution stands for.[77]

Marshall had made all the points that he felt were important to the case. Now all he could do was wait for the justices to weigh the arguments and make their decision. It was to be a long wait. In September 1953 Chief Justice Fred M. Vinson suffered a heart attack and died, delaying the deliberations until a new chief justice could be appointed. The man chosen was former California governor Earl Warren. He assumed the post in October 1953, and deliberations resumed almost immediately.

Marshall and his staff waited nervously for the decision to be announced. He was hoping that his arguments convinced at least five of the justices to vote in his favor. Marshall thought he had argued the cases well and that Justices Earl Warren, William O. Douglas, Hugo L. Black, Sherman Minton, and Harold H. Burton were convinced. But Justices Tom C. Clark, Robert H. Jackson, Stanley F. Reed, who were all southerners, and Justice Felix Frankfurter, who was worried about the effect of desegregation, seemed inclined to vote against him. If just one of the five justices he was counting on changed his mind, Marshall's case would be lost. Marshall was certain none of the southern justices, especially Justice Reed, a conservative Kentuckian, would ever vote to abolish segregation.

Second-Class Citizens

Marshall argued before the Supreme Court that segregation made black students feel like second-class citizens. The following portion of his argument is excerpted from Nancy Whitelaw's Mr. Civil Rights.

"The plain purpose and effect of segregated education is to perpetuate an inferior status for Negroes which is America's sorry heritage from slavery. . . . In the South, where I spend most of my time, you will see white and colored kids going down the road together to school. They separate and go to different schools, and they come out and play together. I do not see why there would necessarily be any trouble if they went to school together. . . . Segregation of Negroes . . . brands the Negro with the mark of inferiority and asserts that he is not fit to associate with white people."

Solidarity

While Marshall waited and worried, the justices were hard at work, trying to draft a final opinion, or written verdict. When it was finally finished, Chief Justice Warren personally delivered a copy of the Court's decision to Justice Jackson, who was critically ill in the hospital. To show the justices' solidarity, Jackson left his hospital bed to be present in the courtroom when the decision was announced on May 17, 1954.

The justices quietly took their places, and solemnly Chief Justice Warren began reading the long-awaited decision:

> In approaching the problem we cannot turn the clock back. . . . We must consider public education in the light of its . . . present place in American life. . . . It is the very foundation of good citizenship; . . . it is doubtful that any child may reasonably be expected to succeed in life if he is denied the opportunity of an education. Such an opportunity . . . is a right which must be made available to all on equal terms. . . . We come then to the question presented: Does segregation of children in public schools solely on the basis of race . . . deprive the children of the minority group of equal educational opportunities? We believe that it does.[78]

Chief Justice Warren felt that it was important to let the country know that the Court stood undivided on the issue of segregation. As he reached the conclusion of the Court's written opinion, he paused and looked up from the documents to face the assembled crowd. He then very deliberately inserted the word *unanimously*, which did not appear in the text, to his closing statement. Warren's words rang out over the hushed courtroom as he stated: "We conclude unanimously that in the field of public education the doctrine of 'separate but equal' has no place. Separate educational facilities are inherently unequal."[79]

When the chief justice said *unanimously*, looks of astonishment crossed the faces of those present. Justice Stanley Reed, who had been the last undecided member of the Court, wept as the opinion was read. Later he told his law clerks that "if it was not the most important decision in the history of the Court, it was very close." Warren noted that while he was reading the Court's decision in *Brown*, "a wave of emotion swept the room; no words or intentional movement, yet a distinct emotional manifestation that defies description."[80]

Reporters, lawyers, and others immediately asked for the dissenting opinions that they were sure the southern justices had written. Even though they were not in complete agreement on how desegregation should proceed, not one of the justices had written a dissension to express his own opinion. The justices felt strongly that to show any division in their ranks would cause great upheaval in the parts of the nation that were against desegregation and turn their landmark ruling into a bitter social war.

It was almost unbelievable to Marshall and to most others that they had been able to bring all nine of the justices over to one side, particularly the southern justices. Marshall later spoke of that amazing moment: "I watched [Reed's] eyes as Warren read the opinion. He was looking me

Marshall stands with fellow lawyers George Hayes (left) and James Nabrit (right) on the steps of the Supreme Court building after the Court's 1954 landmark decision declaring segregation unconstitutional.

right straight in the face too, because he wanted to see my reaction when I realized he hadn't written that dissent."[81]

Marshall was not alone in seeing what a great victory this decision was. Chief Justice Warren gave much of the credit to the three southern justices for having the courage to go against their southern roots. He stated, "They stood right up and did it anyway because they thought it was right." Justice Frankfurter called May 17, 1954, "a day that will live in glory."[82]

Marshall's staff and his NAACP bosses were ecstatic about the *Brown* decision, but Marshall was stoic. He knew that they still had a long way to go. When Marshall's office staff and the other NAACP lawyers held a wild victory celebration,

Marshall just said, "You fools go ahead and have your fun, but we ain't begun to work yet."[83]

Confusion in the South

The South reacted in confusion to the *Brown* decision. Some of the states' governors took the high road, declaring that while not in favor of the Supreme Court's ruling, they would follow the law. Some southern newspapers supported the decision and were optimistic about the future. The Raleigh, North Carolina, *News & Observer* claimed that the ruling "will be met in the South with the good sense and the

The Supreme Court Rules

The following is a partial text of the Supreme Court decision in Brown v. Board of Education, *delivered by Chief Justice Earl Warren on May 17, 1954. The text is excerpted from Maureen Harrison and Steve Gilbert's* Landmark Decisions of the United States Supreme Court.

"We come then to the question presented: Does segregation of children in public schools solely on the basis of race, even though the physical facilities and other 'tangible' factors may be equal, deprive the children of the minority group of equal educational opportunities? We believe that it does.

In *Sweatt v. Painter*, in finding that a segregated law school for Negroes could not provide them equal educational opportunities, this Court relied in large part on 'those qualities which are incapable of objective measurement but which make for greatness in a law school.' In *McLaurin v. Oklahoma State Regents*, the Court, in requiring that a Negro admitted to a white graduate school be treated like all other students, again resorted to intangible consideration: ' . . . his ability to study, to engage in discussions and exchange views with other students, and, in general, to learn his profession.' Such considerations apply with added force to children in grade and high schools. To separate them from others of similar age and qualifications solely because of their race generates a feeling of inferiority as to their status in the community that may affect their hearts and minds in a way unlikely ever to be undone. The effect of this separation on their educational opportunities was well stated by a finding in the Kansas case which nevertheless felt compelled to rule against the Negro plaintiffs:

'Segregation of white and colored children in public schools has a detrimental effect upon the colored children. The impact is greater when it has the sanction of the law. . . . Segregation with the sanction of law . . . has a tendency to [retard] the educational and mental development of Negro children and to deprive them of some of the benefits they would receive in a racial[ly] integrated school system.'

. . . We conclude that in the field of public education the doctrine of 'separate but equal' has no place. Separate educational facilities are inherently unequal."

good will of the people of both races in a manner which will serve the children and honor America." And Greenville, Mississippi's *Delta Democrat-Times* even chided southerners, stating: "If ever a region asked for such a decree the South did through its shocking, calculated and cynical disobedience to its own state constitutions, which specify that separate school systems must be equal."[84]

Others were more begrudging in their acceptance. The Richmond, Virginia, *News Leader* stated: "We accept the Supreme Court's ruling. We do not accept it willingly, or cheerfully or philosophically. We accept it because we have to."[85]

Throughout the South the segregationists were outraged and vowed not to obey the ruling. Some southern newspapers quickly labeled the day Black Monday. Others were ready to go to war to prevent desegregation from occurring. Georgia governor Herman Talmadge declared the Supreme Court had "reduced our Constitution to a mere scrap of paper" and that the state of Georgia would not accept or abide by the Court's "bald political decree without basis in law."[86]

With All Deliberate Speed

On May 31, 1955, the Supreme Court set guidelines for desegregation. The Court ordered all segregated schools to make "a

Students exchange precarious glances at a desegregated southern school at the start of a new school year in 1954.

prompt and reasonable start toward full compliance"[87] with the *Brown* decision. They directed the lower courts to act as monitors of the schools' progress. The only time frame the Court issued was that desegregation was to proceed at "all deliberate speed." Marshall was disappointed in the Court's directive. He felt that the schools should be desegregated immediately and that the Court should clearly state the time frame. Marshall predicted that the Court's soft approach would give the conservative South ample reasons to delay desegregation, for to many southerners, "all deliberate speed" meant never. He was soon proven correct.

On June 1 the editor of the Richmond *News Leader* ridiculed the Supreme Court, calling its members "that inept fraternity of politicians and professors . . . [who] repudiated the Constitution, spit upon the Tenth Amendment [which gives states the right to establish laws], and rewrote the fundamental law of this land to suit their own gauzy concepts of sociology." He urged the South to undertake "a long course of lawful resistance. . . . Let us pledge ourselves to litigate this thing for fifty years."[88] Indeed, the lack of exact deadlines resulted in further litigation, and the desegregation of schools was slowly carried out through the next two decades.

Marshall returned to New York exhausted and depressed. He had spent three years working endless hours on the education cases. During that time, his wife, Buster, had been diagnosed with cancer. She had struggled valiantly but died in February 1955. Biographer Rowan reports that Marshall spoke of "how terrible [it was] just to watch her lie there dying.

Marshall fields questions from the press during a 1955 news conference regarding desegregation.

After the Brown *decision Marshall was frustrated and disappointed that desegregation was being implemented so slowly.*

Every day you'd look at her and she'd gone down further."[89]

Grief consumed Marshall, and he had practically moved into his office to keep from returning to his empty house each night. In the period surrounding Buster's death, Marshall's sadness seemed to be compounded. In March the NAACP executive secretary Walter White died, and his leadership was sorely missed. And with the varied but sometimes angry reactions to the *Brown* verdict, it seemed that the

biggest victory of Marshall's life might tear the South apart.

The Little Rock Nine

Marshall lost himself in his work, dividing his time between the NAACP's New York office and local chapters that needed his help. During this time, one of the most frightening cases Marshall worked on was in the Little Rock, Arkansas, school district. He and NAACP lawyer Wiley Branton worked for over a year to integrate the schools there. They spent many nights at the home of Little Rock NAACP activist Daisy Bates, who was subject to frequent harassment by militant segregationalists. Though nervous, Marshall and Branton made a joke out of who would have to sleep in the bed closest to the window—a window that had already had bricks and homemade firebombs tossed through it.

Finally, in the fall of 1957, Little Rock's all-white Central High School was scheduled to admit nine African-American students. To prevent these students from entering, Arkansas governor Orval E. Faubus ordered the Arkansas National Guard to block all the doors to the school. The students were admitted only after President Dwight D. Eisenhower sent in federal troops to open the doors, escort the African-American students to and from school, and stand guard in the hallways during classes. Attorney General Herbert Brownell said of the situation:

> We felt that this was the test case that had to be made in order to dramatize to everyone that when it came to a showdown the federal government was

Marshall arrives at the U.S. District Court in 1957 to preside over an injunction hearing to permit integration at Central High School in Little Rock, Arkansas.

supreme in this area. The situation was as close as you could get to an irreconcilable difference between the North and the South. There'd been nothing like it since the Civil War.[90]

The battle waged at Central High bore out Marshall's worst fears and shocked the nation. At the end of the school year, Arkansas officials claimed they could not integrate the state's schools without fear of violence and used the Little Rock incident as an example. From Arkansas Marshall once more went to the Supreme Court on September 11, 1958, to fight for

integration. In *Cooper v. Aaron* Marshall argued the case of the Little Rock Nine by stating:

Even if it be claimed that tension will result which will disturb the educational process, this is preferable to the complete breakdown of education which will result from teaching that courts of law will bow to violence; . . . it's only a question of time until integration is completed. We'll solve the problem peacefully—and gradually.[91]

Even while arguing that segregation must end, Marshall knew it would be a long and slow process. While many at the NAACP saw the integration of Central High as a deathblow to segregation in the South, Marshall still voiced caution. When interviewed about the events in Little Rock, Marshall predicted: "In some states—where people wanted to integrate but were afraid of trouble—they may go ahead now that they see they really have the backing of the federal government. . . . In the Deep South, it'll toughen resistance immeasurably."[92]

And Marshall's predictions proved true. Many other school boards and politicians tried evasive plans or scare tactics to keep African-American children from mixing with white children. Eventually southern schools were integrated, but it was many years before African Americans received the equal education they deserved.

Elizabeth Eckford bravely walks by National Guardsmen and heckling students in an effort to enroll in newly desegregated Central High School.

The Law Must Be Enforced

Following the violence against black schoolchildren in Little Rock, Arkansas, Marshall and the NAACP filed a brief stating that the rights of black students must be protected. The following excerpt is taken from Randall Bland's book Private Pressure on Public Law: The Legal Career of Thurgood Marshall.

"Neither overt public resistance, nor the possibility of it, constitutes sufficient cause to nullify the orders of the federal court directing petitioners to proceed with their desegregation plan. This Court and other courts have consistently held that the preservation of the public peace may not be accomplished by interference with rights created by the federal constitution. . . .

Here one state agency, the School Board, seeks to be relieved of its constitutional obligation. . . . To solve this problem by further delaying the constitutional rights of the respondents is unthinkable."

White students at Little Rock Junior High School protest the admission of black students into their school. Such hostilities turned to violence in some cases, causing Marshall and the NAACP to take action to protect black students.

An Uphill Battle

Every right granted to African Americans followed hard-fought legal battles. But because the Supreme Court had used the language that it did in the *Brown* decision, stating that separate facilities were inherently unequal, the NAACP had firm footing to try new cases. Marshall and others in the NAACP spent the years that followed *Brown* trying to make other forms of segregation illegal. By 1963 the Supreme Court had struck down laws that allowed segregation in public buildings, transportation, places of recreation, eating establishments, and housing. The Court declared: "It is no longer open to question that a State may not constitutionally require segregation of public facilities."[93] The *Brown* decision had indeed signaled the end of "separate," but Marshall knew it would be years before African Americans became "equal."

7 Marshall on the Bench

After his victory in the *Brown* case, Marshall continued his work with the NAACP, but after twenty-five years of courtroom battles, he was growing weary. Marshall said he believed of himself: "[I've] outlived my usefulness, in original ideas, in the NAACP hierarchy."[94] It was time to move on to new challenges.

On September 23, 1961, Marshall was called to a new challenge when President John F. Kennedy nominated him to be a judge on the U.S. Court of Appeals for the Second Circuit. President Kennedy was committed to civil rights:

> One hundred years of delay have passed since President Lincoln freed the slaves, yet their heirs, their grandsons are not fully free. They are not yet free from the bonds of injustice, they are not yet free from social and economic oppression, and this nation, for all its hopes and boasts, will not be fully free until all its citizens are free.[95]

Many southern senators were adamantly opposed to Marshall's nomination and succeeded in delaying his appointment until September 1962 by refusing to approve his nomination for an entire year.

When his nomination was finally approved, Marshall plunged into the job. He enjoyed doing the research needed in the

many different areas of law for the various cases that came before him. After so many years of handling civil rights cases, it was refreshing for him to study maritime law or tax law. He was very conscious that as

Marshall sits with members of the Senate Judiciary Subcommittee on the day they approved his nomination to the U.S. Court of Appeals for the Second Circuit.

Marshall enjoyed the stability that his position as a federal judge provided his family, but he missed his activist work. When he was offered the position of solicitor general, he accepted and was once more directly involved in the fight for civil rights.

one of the first African-American federal judges, each of his decisions would be closely scrutinized. Marshall's meticulous attention to each case paid off. Not one of Judge Marshall's 118 decisions was reversed by the U.S. Supreme Court.

A Surprise Call

Marshall enjoyed his place on the federal bench and the security it provided his family. Following Buster's death, Marshall had remarried in 1955 to Cecilia "Cissy" Suyat, a secretary at the NAACP, and the couple had two sons in the seven years following their marriage. But Marshall missed his activist work. He had never been one to sit on the sidelines; he had always been in the thick of the fight. Then on July 12, 1965, while lunching with some courthouse friends, Marshall was

told he had a telephone call from the president. He flippantly replied, "The president of what?"[96] Marshall was speechless when the caller turned out to be the president of the United States, Lyndon B. Johnson, calling to personally offer him the position of solicitor general.

The solicitor general is a powerful and important position in the Department of Justice. This person is the chief appellate lawyer for the government, presenting the government's cases to the Supreme Court. Also, the justices depend on the solicitor general to sort through the thousands of cases they receive each year and weed out those cases that are inappropriate for the Court's attention. The solicitor general is vital to the smooth operation of the Supreme Court and is often referred to as its tenth member.

Marshall was flattered but uncertain whether to accept President Johnson's offer. His federal judgeship was a lifetime appointment. The job of solicitor general had no such guarantee and could be given to someone else if Johnson was not reelected for a second term. Also, the solicitor general's salary was about forty-five hundred dollars less than his salary as a federal judge. As a judge Marshall was forced to take an impartial view of cases that were presented to him. However, as solicitor general, Marshall would no longer be bound to sit on the sidelines. Once more he could be an active proponent, or advocate, for the cases he was working with. He would also be able to join the fight for civil rights again.

Johnson's Secret Plan

Secretly President Johnson had big plans for Marshall. Johnson wanted to appoint an African American to the Supreme Court, and he thought Marshall was the perfect candidate. The president confided to an aide that he considered Marshall

> a lawyer and judge of very high ability. A patriot of deep conviction, and a gentleman of undisputed integrity. . . . I'm going to take Thurgood, and I'm going to make him solicitor general, and then when somebody says, "He doesn't have a lot of experience for the Supreme Court," . . . [he] will have prosecuted more cases before the Supreme Court than any lawyer in America. So how's anybody gonna turn him down?[97]

Johnson knew how much Marshall loved to be in the middle of the fray and persuaded him that he could do more for civil rights as solicitor general than he

ever could as a federal judge. Marshall later commented that by the end of his conversation with Johnson,

> I was ashamed that I hadn't volunteered [for the position]. LBJ is a convincing gentleman. . . . Negroes have made great advances in government and I think it's time they started making some sacrifices. I accepted because the President of the United States asked and, secondly, the President who asked was Lyndon Johnson, who has demonstrated his leadership in civil rights. When he asks you to be a part of what he is doing to give full equality to Negroes, the least you can do is help.[98]

Marshall expected the same long wait and mudslinging that he had faced before his federal judgeship appointment was confirmed. To his delighted surprise he was interviewed for less than half an hour by five friendly senators. With no hostile debates and no delaying tactics, Marshall became solicitor general on August 11, 1965.

President Johnson was very proud that Marshall had accepted the position of solicitor general. The president often spoke of "how gratifying it was for school children to know that when the great United States Government spoke in the highest court in the land it did so through a Negro."[99]

Solicitor General Marshall

During his term as solicitor general, Marshall argued nineteen cases before the Supreme Court, winning fourteen of them. He was especially concerned with shaping the role that the courts would play in administering justice in accordance with the new civil rights laws. Before these laws were passed, state courts often would refuse to bring to trial white defendants who were accused of committing crimes against African Americans. Under the new civil rights laws, however, if a crime such as murder could be shown to be racially motivated, then it could be called a civil rights crime. Civil rights crimes could be tried in a federal court rather than a state court. Marshall felt that it was important to establish this distinction so that crimes committed against African Americans in the South would not go unpunished.

For example, in a case in Philadelphia, Mississippi, three black civil rights volunteers were lynched. A Mississippi grand jury dismissed the charges, because the accused were white law enforcement officers. Marshall was furious. As solicitor general, he convinced the Supreme Court to reinstate the indictments and to hear the case as a civil rights case. As a result, seven men were convicted. This was the first time in Mississippi's history that a white person had ever been convicted for a crime against an African American. Solicitor General Marshall established the far-reaching power behind the new civil rights laws and, more importantly, showed the South that justice would be done.

Marshall's family and President Johnson look on as Marshall takes his oath as solicitor general in 1965.

The Right Time and the Right Man

Although Marshall enjoyed his position as solicitor general, he was soon on the move again. Supreme Court Justice Tom C. Clark announced his decision to retire, and on June 13, 1967, President Johnson announced his nomination of Thurgood Marshall as an associate justice of the Supreme Court. Johnson said, "I believe he earned that appointment. He deserves the appointment. He is the best qualified by training and by very valuable service to the country. I believe it is the right thing

Solicitor General

While some conservative critics felt that Marshall's ties to the NAACP might make him biased, the Senate committee that interviewed Thurgood Marshall for the position of solicitor general of the United States publicly denounced those concerns. The following statement, excerpted from the Senate Judiciary Committee records, was made by Congressman William Ryan of New York in support of Marshall.

"Judge Marshall is uniquely qualified for this responsibility. He has argued more than a score of cases in the Supreme Court and other Federal courts and has been successful on almost every occasion. In the 32 cases which he has argued before the Nation's highest tribunal—before which he will have to appear as Solicitor General—he has established the remarkable record of winning 29. This is a record of which any practicing lawyer could be very proud.

I personally and most Americans applaud the contribution he has made to our jurisprudence [legal system] in his 20 years as chief counsel of the NAACP. Regardless of individual feelings, his skills are universally recognized. . . .

Although the leading civil rights lawyer of his time, his 4 years on the bench have demonstrated that he is a lawyer's judge, and an American, not a special pleader for any group or segment of the country. . . .

At the time of his nomination to the Federal bench, allegations impugning [attacking] his patriotism were circulated. The extensive inquiry made by the committee, his overwhelming confirmation by the Senate, and his exemplary performance as a judge extinguished even the most unreasonable of these charges. Nevertheless, in the past few days, false charges have appeared anew in the Congressional Record. I deplore, as I am sure the members of this distinguished committee deplore, the attempt to malign a great American."

President Johnson announces his nomination of Marshall as an associate justice of the Supreme Court in 1967.

to do, the right time to do it, the right man and the right place."[100]

Many members of Congress spoke out in support of Marshall's confirmation. Montana senator Mike Mansfield said, "Thurgood Marshall's rise to the Supreme Court reaffirms the American ideal that what counts is what you are and not who you are, or whom your [parents] may have been." Senator Thomas H. Kuchel, a Republican from California, said that Thurgood Marshall's ascent to the Supreme Court was "part of a larger process in which not only Negro Americans but Americans from all minority racial and religious backgrounds have

begun to participate in the affairs of the nation."[101]

There was also popular support for Marshall outside the government and the legal community. G. Theodore Mitau, the chancellor of the Minnesota state college system at the time, stated:

I would say he was uniquely qualified for the appointment, . . . particularly at a time when the Court is confronted with some of the reverberations of the black revolution. There can be little doubt that his appointment has given the reasonable and moderate leadership among the blacks significant and

Supreme Court Justice

Marshall's nomination for Supreme Court justice was placed before the Senate Judiciary Committee by Robert F. Kennedy, U.S. senator from the state of New York. In his nomination speech, Kennedy highlighted Marshall's varied background and the breadth of knowledge he could bring to the Supreme Court. The following portion is excerpted from the records of the U.S. Senate Judiciary Committee.

"In nominating Judge Marshall, President Johnson has selected for our highest court a man who brings with him not only a long and distinguished career of . . . legal experience, but also a man whose work has symbolized and spearheaded the struggle of millions of Americans for equality before the law.

. . . I have known him for some period of time, and have the greatest respect for him. Mr. Chairman and members of the committee, I know what a fine judge he made, and I know what an outstanding job he did as Solicitor General of the United States. I know he is a man of integrity and a man of honesty, and a man of ability, and I commend him to the committee."

Robert F. Kennedy (far right), shown with Marshall and Senator Jacob Javits of New York, praised Marshall during his nomination speech, calling him "a man of integrity and a man of honesty."

Justice Marshall poses with his family outside the Supreme Court building in Washington following his swearing-in ceremonies.

tangible evidence of having one of their people attain the high honor and power that membership on the Court denotes.[102]

But not everyone supported Marshall's appointment. Marshall was a liberal, and many conservatives thought that he would automatically favor individuals' rights over those of the state, criminals' rights over victims, the poor over the rich, and minorities' rights above all.

During confirmation hearings, the conservative members of Congress played on those fears by asking Marshall pointed questions such as, "Mr. Solicitor General, isn't it true that you were responsible for getting the Supreme Court to favor our criminals by restricting the use of voluntary confessions?"[103] Senators from Arkansas, North and South Carolina, and West Virginia posed question after question, many on obscure points of law, portraying Marshall as unqualified for a seat on the Court. Some of the questions were trivial or obscure to the point of being ridiculous, such as, "Of what significance do you believe it is that in deciding the constitutional basis of the Civil Rights Act of 1866, Congress copied the enforcement provisions of this legislation from the Fugitive Slave Law of 1850?"[104]

Justice Marshall

It was not until August 30 that the committee finished questioning Marshall and submitted his nomination to the entire Senate. It was approved immediately by a vote of sixty-nine to eleven. The Senate committee's addition to its final report read:

> There probably has never been any nominee for any judicial position who has received more minute and searching examination. . . . The Senate will do itself honor, the Court will be graced, and the nation benefited by our confirmation of this nominee to the Supreme Court.[105]

Both President Johnson and Marshall were relieved. They had anticipated a longer battle with the southern senators and several weeks of questioning. Instead, Thurgood Marshall was about to become the first African American to wear the robes of a U.S. Supreme Court justice. Johnson proudly told reporters:

> When I appointed Thurgood Marshall to the Supreme Court, I figured he'd be a great example to younger kids. There was probably not a Negro in America who didn't know about Thurgood's appointment. All over America that day Negro parents looked at their children a little differently, thousands of mothers looked across the breakfast table and said: "Now maybe this will happen to my child someday."[106]

On September 1, 1967, Thurgood Marshall was sworn in, with his wife, Cissy, and his sons, Thurgood Jr. and John William, watching proudly. Marshall sent out a formal written statement that said:

> [I am] greatly honored by the appointment and its confirmation. . . . Let me take this opportunity to reaffirm my deep faith in this nation and its people and to pledge that I shall be ever mindful of my obligation to the Constitution and to the goal of equal justice under law.[107]

The Committee Approves

The Senate Judiciary Committee approved the nomination of Thurgood Marshall on August 21, 1967. The following excerpt from the committee's report is quoted from Roy M. Mersky and J. Myron Jacobstein's The Supreme Court.

"The nominee twice before has been considered for Presidential nominations by this committee. In the history of the Senate there probably has never been any nominee for any judicial position who has received more minute and searching examination. The nominee's appearances before two subcommittees of the Judiciary Committee and now the full Judiciary Committee have been most revealing. The very curtain of his soul has been parted its full width opening to view his character, his philosophy, and the quality of his judicial temperament. This view, at this critical point in time, has shown Judge Marshall's unique qualification to sit on the Nation's highest court and to enforce her law and protect her Constitution fairly, fully and faithfully. The committee after full consideration has recommended Judge Marshall for confirmation."

Members of the U.S. Supreme Court in 1967. Marshall would spend his years on the bench trying to uphold the Constitution and ensure social justice for all people.

But when asked by author and friend Carl Rowan how it felt to be joining the Court, Marshall beamed and said, "How did I feel? Hell, like any lawyer in America would feel. Real proud—because there is no greater honor a lawyer can get. I felt especially great because I knew President Johnson was using me to say something important to the nation."[108]

One of the Brethren

As Marshall took his place on the Court, he was asked by reporters about his philos-

ophy of law. Everyone knew his feelings about civil rights, but no one could predict how that might affect the decisions he would be making on the Court. Marshall answered that all his life he had been an unshakable believer in the power of the Constitution to grant all the people all their rights. Marshall said:

> The Constitution has to meet the different needs of a different society. . . . I think it's the greatest body of laws ever, and what to me and to many people is so extraordinary about it is that in this late day you find that it works, and when you dig down into it,

I don't know of any better job that could have been done. . . . If you read it with any understanding, there's hardly anything that it doesn't cover. It's unbelievable that a Constitution written in the horse and buggy days would cover outer space.[109]

Marshall called the Constitution a living document, whose words must be interpreted in light of life today, not life when it was written. He pointed out that his views were not new to the Court, quoting the very first Supreme Court chief justice, John Marshall, who said that the Constitution was intended to endure for ages and to be adapted to human needs. These are the beliefs that Thurgood Marshall took with him when he joined his brethren, as the Court justices called themselves, on the Supreme Court.

8 The Supreme Court Years

When Marshall joined the Supreme Court, he enjoyed being part of a group in which most of his brethren shared his basic views on social equality and personal rights. During his early years as a justice, Marshall found himself voting with his fellow justices to expand civil rights and personal liberty.

The Freedom of Speech

Many of the cases the Court heard during these years concerned the First Amendment right to freedom of speech and expression. During the initial part of Marshall's term, the Court was overrun with pornography cases. Many cities wanted to ban so-called dirty movies or magazines. The makers and distributors of the movies and publications claimed they were exercising their right to freedom of expression. In 1957 the Court had ruled that obscenity was not protected by the First Amendment. Now the Court had to rule on each of these cases individually by viewing the offending material to decide whether it was obscene. But the Court had no real guidelines to define obscenity. Some, like Justices Black and Douglas, believed that there should never be any re-

strictions on speech, writing, or art. Other justices felt that erotic movies or any type of pornography were not examples of free speech and thus were not protected by the First Amendment. Justice Potter Stewart said it was difficult to define obscenity, "but I know it when I see it."[110]

Cecilia Marshall buttons her husband's robe as Marshall begins his first term as Supreme Court justice.

In dealing with the obscenity cases, Marshall became acquainted with the process of writing opinions. Each justice is allowed to write an explanation, called an opinion, to explain the choice of concurring in or dissenting from the majority ruling of the Court.

In the 1968 case of *Interstate Circuit, Inc. v. City of Dallas*, Marshall wrote his first majority opinion. The case concerned city leaders in Dallas who had appointed a board to review movies and decide whether people under sixteen would be allowed to see them. When the board banned an erotic film, its makers appealed to the Supreme Court. In his opinion Marshall noted that while banning a movie in Dallas would not put Hollywood out of business or change the kind of films that they made, he had to keep the bigger picture in mind. For whatever the Court allowed the city of Dallas to restrict, it must also allow all other cities to restrict. Acknowledging this, Marshall voted against Dallas, saying that the city's ordinance that banned the film was too broad and too vague and that it violated the filmmakers' First Amendment right to freedom of expression.

When the First Amendment was involved, Marshall was clear and to the point about his beliefs. In the 1968 case of *Pickering v. Board of Education*, Marshall addressed the injustice of a teacher's being fired for writing a letter that criticized the school board. Marshall said, "Teachers are, as a class, the members of a community most likely to have informed and definite opinions . . . [about] the operation of the schools. . . . Accordingly, it is essential that they be able to speak out freely . . . without fear of dismissal."[111]

Soon Marshall's commonsense style began to make its mark. In the 1969 *Stanley v. Georgia* case, the Court ruled that individuals were guaranteed the right to read or watch whatever they wished in their own homes, even if the material was deemed obscene. Justice Marshall stated:

> If the First Amendment means anything, it means that a state has no business telling a man, . . . what books he may read or what films he may watch. Our whole constitutional heritage rebels at the thought of giving government the power to control men's minds.[112]

Justice Douglas called Marshall's opinions the "only remotely rational development"[113] in the obscenity cases since the Court had begun hearing them.

Marshall Makes an Impression

Marshall made an impression on his fellow justices with his stinging dissents as well. Dissenting in the 1972 case of *Adams v. Williams*, which allowed police officers the right to stop and search suspects, he warned:

> The Fourth Amendment, which was included in the Bill of Rights to prevent this kind of arbitrary and oppressive police action . . . is dealt a serious blow. Today's decision invokes [brings forth] the specter [haunting vision] of a society in which innocent citizens may be stopped, searched, and arrested at the whim of police officers who have only the slightest suspicion of improper conduct.[114]

In the 1972 *Furman v. Georgia* case, Marshall wrote one of his most moving opinions, agreeing with the five-to-four vote that capital punishment—the death penalty—was "cruel and unusual" punishment. He said:

> At times a cry is heard that morality requires vengeance. . . . But the Eighth Amendment is our insulation from our baser selves. The "cruel and unusual" language limits . . . vengeance. . . . [If this were not so], . . . a return to the rack and other tortures would be possible. . . . [Capital punishment] is morally unacceptable. . . . The burden of capital punishment falls upon the poor, the ignorant, and the underprivileged members of society, . . . who are least able to voice their complaints. . . . Their impotence leaves them victims of a [punishment] that the wealthier, better-represented, just-as-guilty person can escape.[115]

Marshall was well respected by the other justices. They appreciated his insight and his experience with the poor and oppressed and his ability to communicate those experiences to his fellow justices. Justice William J. Brennan Jr. said of Marshall:

> I don't think there's anyone in the country who can match either his experience or his expression of his experience. . . . When he . . . puts himself to it, the . . . product is just as good as it used to be in his trial days, when he was regarded—and with justification—as one of the ablest trial lawyers in the country.[116]

In deciding the cases brought before the Court, Marshall remained dedicated

Like many of the other justices, William J. Brennan was impressed by Marshall's depth of experience and his ability to relate to the poor and oppressed.

to following the intent of the Constitution and the Bill of Rights. After years of presenting cases in courts across the country, Marshall was a quick thinker who liked to listen quietly as cases were presented, then fire precise, straightforward questions at the defense counsel. When discussing the cases in the Court's private chambers, Marshall enjoyed the give-and-take of ideas with the other justices. He was always himself, relaxed and plainspoken, never intimidated by his surroundings or the other justices. Marshall knew his own heart and "saw his job as casting his vote and urging his colleagues to do what was right."[117]

The Mood of the Court Shifts

When Marshall joined the Court in 1967, most of his fellow justices shared his basic beliefs, and he seldom needed to urge his brethren to his way of thinking. At that time the Court, called the Warren Court after Chief Justice Earl Warren, was known as a liberal Court. Marshall was in the majority, but within five years the balance had shifted toward a more conservative Court. As some of the older justices left, they were replaced by conservative appointees selected by conservative presidents. These new justices did not share Marshall's views on issues such as freedom of speech, the right to privacy, capital punishment, or discrimination against minorities.

Marshall watched his fellow liberals leave the Court in rapid succession. When Chief Justice Warren retired in 1969, President Richard M. Nixon selected Warren E. Burger to take his place. Burger was a U.S. Court of Appeals judge and was very conservative. Also in 1969, Justice Abe Fortas stepped down and was replaced by conservative Harry A. Blackmun. Justices Hugo L. Black and John Marshall Harlan retired in 1971, and Nixon appointed Lewis F. Powell Jr. and William H. Rehnquist, both conservatives, to the Court. Marshall soon found himself and Justice Brennan as the sole defenders of many of the rights that the Court had ruled in favor of years earlier.

As the Court became more conservative, Marshall saw his role as that of a watchdog for the people who he felt had little voice in lawmaking—the poor, people of color, women, and the criminally accused. Marshall always spoke out on the side of personal rights and individual freedom and voiced his frustrations at the Court's new conservative stance through a series of stinging dissenting opinions. By the end of his Supreme Court career, Marshall had written over eighteen hundred dissents, more than any of his colleagues. In these dissents Marshall voiced his growing frustration with his conservative colleagues.

Watchdog of the Court

Marshall's first battle with his brethren came in the 1970 *James v. Valtierra* case, which dealt with discrimination against the poor. In his dissenting opinion Marshall wrote:

> It is far too late in the day to contend that the Fourteenth Amendment prohibits only racial discrimination; and to me, singling out the poor to bear a burden not placed on any other class of citizens tramples the values the Fourteenth Amendment was designed to protect. [118]

Marshall spoke out on behalf of the poor, again, in the 1973 case of *United States v. Kras.* In this case Marshall demonstrated the depth of his experience and his own personal knowledge of poverty. The majority had ruled that a fifty-dollar fee did not prevent the poor from filing for bankruptcy, saying that Kras and others like him could pay the fee in weekly installments. Marshall used his dissent to educate his fellow justices on what poverty really meant. He wrote:

> It may be easy for some people to think that weekly savings of less than

two dollars are no burden. But no one who has had close contact with poor people can fail to understand how close to the margin of survival many of them are. A sudden illness, for example, may destroy whatever savings they may have accumulated. . . . A pack or two of cigarettes may be, for them, not a routine purchase but a luxury indulged in only rarely. The desperately poor almost never go to see a movie, which the majority seems to believe is an almost weekly activity. . . . [It] is disgraceful for an interpretation of the Constitution to be premised upon unfounded assumptions about how people live. [119]

As the Court became more conservative in the 1970s, Marshall regarded himself as one of the few voices for minorities, women, and the poor.

Protecting the Rights of All

Marshall spoke out on any case in which he felt individual rights were being threatened, even when he found himself championing politically unpopular causes like fighting for the rights of the accused. Marshall often found his dissenting opinions the lone voice arguing on behalf of the accused, as in 1970, when addressing the issue of forced confessions. Marshall bluntly stated:

> I had thought that more recent decisions of this Court would have made it abundantly clear that a confession obtained under the circumstances present here [the accused had been beaten so badly that he required brain surgery] would be involuntary and constitutionally inadmissible. [120]

Again and again Marshall berated his colleagues for ignoring the rights of the accused. When the Court decided in 1973 that it was impractical to require police to inform suspects of their right to refuse a search of their property, Marshall wrote a blistering dissent:

> [When] the Court speaks of practicality, what it really is talking about is the continued ability of police to capitalize on the ignorance of citizens. . . . Of course it would be "practical" for the police to ignore . . . the Fourth Amendment, if by practicality we mean that more criminals will be

apprehended, even though the constitutional rights of innocent people also go by the board. . . . The framers of the Fourth Amendment struck the balance against this sort of convenience and in favor of certain basic civil rights. It is not for the Court to restrike that balance because of its own views of the needs of law-enforcement officers.[121]

As the years passed, Marshall grew increasingly discouraged with the direction the Burger Court was taking. He felt that the progress that had been made in civil rights and equality for all people was slowly being destroyed. Marshall said, "It is difficult to characterize these decisions as . . . anything other than a retrenching [reduction] of the civil rights agenda. In the past 35 years, we truly have come full circle."[122]

When conservative Ronald Reagan was elected president in 1980, Marshall saw it as a sign that the country was becoming more conservative and that there would be further attack on the rights that he vowed to protect. Marshall's law clerk, Stephen L. Carter, described the effect that the election had on Marshall. Carter related that Marshall met his friend Justice Brennan in a hall:

Mr. Marshall, towering over his friend, looked down, hesitated, then slipped his arm around Mr. Bren-

Desegregation Is Not an Easy Task

Justice Marshall's dismay is evident in his dissent in the 1974 school desegregation case of Milliken v. Bradley. *The following excerpt is from Roger Goldman's book* Thurgood Marshall: Justice for All.

"Desegregation is not and was never expected to be an easy task. Racial attitudes ingrained in our Nation's childhood and adolescence are not quickly thrown aside in its middle years. But just as the inconvenience of some cannot be allowed to stand in the way of the rights of others, so public opposition, no matter how strident [loud], cannot be permitted to divert this Court from the enforcement of the constitutional principles at issue in this case. Today's holding [ruling], I fear, is more a reflection of a perceived public mood that we have gone far enough in enforcing the Constitution's guarantee of equal justice than it is the product of neutral principles of law. In the short run, it may seem to be the easier course to allow our great metropolitan areas to be divided up each into two cities—one white, the other black—but it is a course, I predict, our people will ultimately regret. I dissent."

During Ronald Reagan's administration, Marshall feared that some of the advances that had been made toward social equality were slipping away.

nan's narrow shoulders. They walked to the robing room that way, passing in and out of the shadows where the brilliant morning sunlight struck curtains or walls. That is the moment when the era ended, as these two great soldiers of liberalism squared their shoulders and marched off to fight their battle against the new political order.[123]

Marshall was so outraged by many of President Reagan's policies that he publicly criticized the president, something a Supreme Court justice—a judge who was supposed to stay removed from politics—had never done in the history of the Court. During a television interview with author Carl T. Rowan, Marshall went so far as to say that he ranked Reagan "at the bottom" of the list of presidents who had helped civil rights. Marshall went on to say:

Everybody quotes Martin Luther King as saying, "Thank God, we're free at last." We're not free, we're nowhere near free. Years ago a Pullman [train] porter told me that he'd been in every state and every city in the country and he'd never been anyplace in this country where he had [to] put his hand up and [feel] his face to know that he was a Negro. I agree with him. Segregation in general, we still have it. I know that there are clubs here in this town [Washington, D.C.] that invite everybody else but me. I don't have an honorary membership in any club in any place under any circumstances.[124]

"Getting Old and Falling Apart"

Marshall continued his fight throughout the 1980s until he physically could fight no more. Worn out and frail after twenty-four years on the bench, Marshall was ready to rest. Finally, on June 27, 1991, he sent notice of his retirement to President George Bush. Marshall cited his age and health as his reasons for stepping down, telling reporters, "I'm getting old and falling apart." [125]

Even though he was retiring, Marshall used his last dissenting opinion in 1991 to voice his disillusionment with his fellow justices. In speaking out once more against the death penalty, Marshall wrote:

> Power, not reason, is the new currency of this Court's decision making. . . . Cast aside today are those condemned to face society's ultimate penalty [the death penalty]. Tomorrow's victims [of the loss of civil rights] may be minorities, women, or the indigent [im-

Health concerns prompted Marshall, pictured with his wife in the late 1980s, to retire from the bench in 1991.

A Living Document

The San Francisco Patent and Trademark Law Association invited Justice Marshall to speak at its annual seminar. During his May 1987 speech to the group in Maui, Hawaii, Marshall explained his belief that the two-hundred-year-old Constitution is a living document. The following is excerpted from James Haskins's Thurgood Marshall: A Life for Justice.

"I do not believe that the meaning of the Constitution was forever 'fixed' at the Philadelphia [Constitutional] Convention [in 1787]. Nor do I find the wisdom, foresight and sense of justice exhibited by the Framers particularly profound. To the contrary, the government they devised was defective from the start, requiring several amendments, a civil war and momentous social transformation to attain the system of constitutional government, and its respect for the individual freedoms and human rights, we hold as fundamental today. . . . The effects of the Framers' compromises had remained for generations. They arose from the contradiction between guaranteeing liberty and justice to all, and denying both to Negroes. . . . [If you have a] sensitive understanding of the Constitution's inherent defects, and its promising evolution through 200 years of history, the celebration of the 'Miracle at Philadelphia' will, in my view, be a far more meaningful and humbling experience. . . . We will see that the true miracle was not the birth of the Constitution but its life, a life nurtured through two turbulent centuries of our own making. . . . Thus, in this bicentennial year, we may not all participate in the festivities with flag-waving fervor. Some may more quietly commemorate the suffering, struggle, and sacrifice that have triumphed over much of what was wrong with the original document, and observe the anniversary with hopes not realized and promises not fulfilled. I plan to celebrate the bicentennial of the Constitution as a living document, including the Bill of Rights and other amendments protecting individual freedoms and human rights."

poverished]. Inevitably this campaign . . . will squander the authority and the legitimacy of this court as a protector of the powerless.[126]

Some conservatives were happy to see Justice Marshall's retirement. But many more people, conservative and liberal, white and African American, were

After announcing his retirement, Marshall addresses reporters during a Supreme Court news conference. Both conservatives and liberals were saddened to see the respected justice step down.

saddened by his departure. Professor Alan Dershowitz of Harvard said:

> The Marshall era was characterized by a vindication of the rights of the downtrodden, the underdog, the minority and the unpopular. It was personified by the only Justice in American history whose entire distinguished career at the bar was in the service of the poor, the disenfranchised and the victims of discrimination.[127]

Civil rights supporters believed that without Justice Marshall on the bench,

some of the hard-won legislation would begin to be reexamined. Linda Greenhouse, writer for the *New York Times*, summed up the mood of many people when Marshall announced his retirement from the Supreme Court. She wrote:

> Thurgood Marshall . . . knows the Court's potential as an instrument for social change better than almost anyone who has ever served there. Even in advanced age, in evident anger and sorrow, his continued presence on the bench made him a powerful symbol of

The Future of Civil Rights

Marshall voiced his opinion of the Burger Court and his view of the future of civil rights in the March 1990 USA Today *article "The Supreme Court and Civil Rights: Has the Tide Turned?"*

"For many years, no institution of American government has been as close a friend to civil rights as the United States Supreme Court. . . . However, we must recognize that the Court's approach to civil rights cases has changed markedly. Its recent opinions vividly illustrate this changed judicial attitude. . . . [It] is difficult to characterize these [recent] decisions as a product of anything other than a retrenching of the civil rights agenda. In the past 35 years, we truly have come full circle. . . . The important question now is where the civil rights struggle should go from here.

One answer, I suppose, is nowhere at all—to stay put. With the school desegregation and voting rights cases and the passage of Federal anti-discrimination statutes [laws], the argument goes, the principal civil rights battles already have been won . . . and we can trust the Supreme Court to ensure that they remain so. . . . [But] we must avoid complacency. . . . The Court's decisions during the 1988–89 term put at risk not only the civil rights of minorities, but of all citizens. History teaches that, when the Supreme Court has been willing to shortchange the equal rights of minority groups, other basic personal civil liberties like the rights to free speech and personal security against unreasonable searches and seizures also are threatened.

Let me emphasize that, while we need not and should not give up on the Supreme Court and while Federal litigation on civil rights issues still can succeed, in the 1990s, we must broaden our perspective. . . . Paraphrasing President Kennedy, those who wish to assure the continued protection of important civil rights should 'ask not what the Supreme Court alone can do for civil rights; ask what you can do to help the course of civil rights.' Today, the answer to that question lies in bringing pressure to bear on all branches [of government], including the Court, and urging them to undertake the battles for civil liberties that remain to be won. With that goal as our guide, we can go forward together to advance civil rights and liberty rights with the fervor we have shown in the past."

the era when the Court demonstrated that potential to a remarkable degree. His departure crystallizes a moment when a historic tide, long in the ebbing, has finally run out and a new history of uncertain dimension has begun to unfold.[128]

Marshall shared these fears and spoke of the ongoing battle for social equality and personal rights in one of his last public appearances as the guest of honor at Philadelphia's Fourth of July celebration in 1992. In his address, Marshall discussed the work still to be done:

The battle has not yet been won; we have barely begun. Americans can do better. . . . America has no choice but to do better to assure justice for all Americans, Afro and white, rich and poor, educated and illiterate. . . . [Our] futures are bound together. . . . I wish I could say that racism and prejudice were only distant memories . . . and that liberty and equality were just around the bend. I wish I could say that America has come to appreciate diversity and to see and accept similarity. But as I look around, I see not a nation of unity but of division. . . . But there is a price to be paid for division and isolation. . . . We cannot play ostrich. Democracy cannot flourish amid fear. Liberty cannot bloom amid hate. Justice cannot take root amid rage. . . . We must go against the prevailing wind. . . . We must dissent because America can do better, because America has no choice but to do better.[129]

Chapter

9 The Marshall Legacy

The compelling voice of Thurgood Marshall was stilled forever on January 24, 1993, when he died of heart failure at the National Naval Medical Center in Bethesda, Maryland. Shortly before his death Marshall said he wanted to be remembered as a man who did what he could with what he had. These humble words give little evidence of the magnitude of the work he accomplished.

During his life, Marshall became the spirit of the civil rights movement. Author Carl T. Rowan assessed Marshall's life by saying, "Throughout six decades, Marshall . . . [was] a demanding spirit of freedom, a sort of ghost inside . . . [segregated] schools, and on buses and trains, in theaters and restaurants where African Americans once were insulted with impunity [without punishment]."[130] Marshall is remembered as a man who devoted his life to the civil rights movement, whose work helped end segregation in America, and who shaped a generation of civil rights crusaders to continue his work.

Justice Sandra Day O'Connor, a justice who often disagreed with Marshall when they served together on the Supreme Court from 1981 to 1991, wrote a tribute to Marshall that echoes Rowan's words:

His was the eye of a lawyer who saw the deepest wounds in the social fabric and used law to heal them. His was the ear of a counselor who understood the vulnerabilities of the accused and established safeguards for their protection. His was the mouth of a man who knew the anguish of the silenced and gave them a voice.[131]

A Nation Mourns

Evidence of the number of people whose lives Marshall's work touched could be seen in the crowds who came to say good-bye to the civil rights leader. Close to twenty thousand mourners waited for hours in bitterly cold weather outside the Supreme Court Building where Marshall's body lay in state on January 27, 1993. The group included politicians and taxi drivers, the very rich and the very poor, and people of all colors and backgrounds. All had come to say good-bye to a hero. The group's feelings were summed up by Cheryl Boone, a Columbia University School of Law student, who was one of the mourners. "The cold [weather] doesn't matter at all," Boone said. "Justice

Marshall was a hero to us, to all black people—and not just to black people, but to all people. . . . He inspired me. He made me believe that everyone has an obligation to society—everyone."[132]

More than four thousand people attended Marshall's funeral at Washington's National Cathedral on January 28, 1993. Among the mourners were President Bill Clinton, twelve current and former Supreme Court justices, members of Congress, and civil rights leaders. Across the country magazines and newspapers mourned the loss of the retired justice and recounted Marshall's impressive record.

Even though Marshall had always chosen the role of defender of individual rights and frequently found himself on the side of the underdog, he usually emerged from his battles victorious. When Marshall left the bench, retired justice William J. Brennan Jr. said of Marshall's record:

Mourners pass Marshall's flag-draped coffin in the Great Hall of the Supreme Court. Nearly twenty thousand people waited in line to pay their last respects to the civil rights leader.

His Influence Lives On

Following Thurgood Marshall's retirement Justice Sandra Day O'Connor wrote a tribute to Marshall in the June 1992 issue of the Stanford University Law Review. *The following portion is excerpted from Carl Rowan's* Dream Makers, Dream Breakers: The World of Justice Thurgood Marshall.

"At oral arguments and conference meetings, in opinions and dissents, Justice Marshall imparted not only his legal acumen but also his life experiences, pushing and prodding us to respond not only to the persuasiveness of legal arguments but also to the power of moral truth.

I have perhaps been most affected by him as a raconteur [storyteller]. In my early months as the junior justice, I looked forward to these tales as diversions from the heavy, often troublesome, task of deciding the complex legal issues before us. But over time, I realized that behind most of these anecdotes was a relevant legal point.

Justice Marshall's experiences are inspiring not only because of what they reveal about him but also because of what they instill in, and ask of, us. . . . That Justice Marshall never hid from prejudice but thrust himself into its midst has been an encouragement and challenge to me."

He leaves behind an enviable record of opinions supporting the rights of the less powerful and less fortunate. One can add that, for more than twenty-five years before he joined the judiciary, Thurgood Marshall was probably the most important advocate in America, one who used his formidable legal skills to end the ills of discrimination. . . . Of no other lawyer can it so truly be said that all Americans owe him an enormous debt of gratitude. [133]

An advocate, a litigator, and a dedicated defender of personal rights, Marshall's work completely changed the constitutional landscape in the area of equal protection under the laws, according to Supreme Court chief justice William Rehnquist during his eulogy for Marshall. [134] When Marshall was born, the world was segregated, and African Americans were denied most of the rights they were entitled to under the Constitution. Marshall dedicated his life to winning African Americans the rights they were promised, and the fruits of his labor live on after his death. Marshall's work to abolish segregation resulted in schools that are open to all. Jim Crow laws have been struck down, and there are generations of children who have never known the feeling of being forced to sit at the back of the

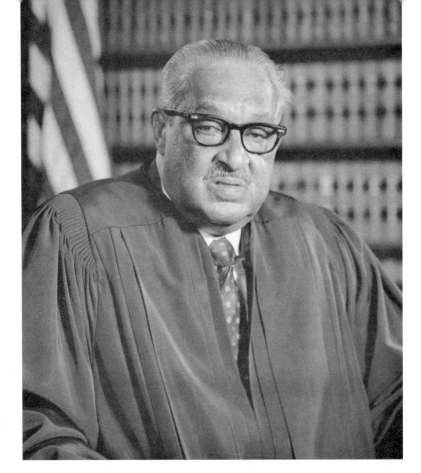

By dedicating his life to fighting for civil rights, Thurgood Marshall made an important and lasting contribution to American society.

bus or being refused service because of the color of their skin.

"We gained our freedoms through the court system, thanks to him," said Commander Mike Taylor, a high-ranking black naval officer who was interviewed by the *Washington Post* after attending Marshall's memorial service. "He was the doorman. He stood there and opened up the door for us and made us set our sights higher."[135]

The Battle Continues

One of Marshall's most important legacies is the numbers of social engineers that he inspired and trained. Marshall left behind a generation of young lawyers to continue his work. His battles "inspired a whole cadre [group] of lawyers to take on that social engineering concept, using the law as an instrument of change,"[136] said Edward Hailes Jr., an NAACP lawyer who was also interviewed by the *Washington Post* after attending Marshall's funeral. Harvard Law School professor and former Marshall clerk Randall L. Kennedy said:

It seems to me that Marshall worked as an advance guard. First, he was very much a disrupter and a rebel. Then others took over that position, and he became an advance guard at being a black American insider at very high levels of government. At each point, he has been a pioneer, opening doors that others have gone through behind him. [137]

While the next generation works to bring social equality through the courts, Marshall's cautionary but hopeful words guide them. In his 1992 Fourth of July address, Marshall issued his final challenge to America:

The legal system can force open doors, and sometimes, even knock down walls. But it cannot build bridges. That job belongs to you and me. We can run from each other but we cannot escape each other. We will only attain freedom if we learn to appreciate what is different and muster the courage to discover what is fundamentally the same. Take a chance, won't you? Knock down the fences that divide. Tear apart the walls that imprison. Reach out; freedom lies just on the other side. [138]

Notes

Introduction: Mr. Civil Rights

1. Quoted in D. J. Herda, *Thurgood Marshall: Civil Rights Champion.* Springfield, NJ: Enslow, 1995, p. 98.

Chapter 1: Shaping a Leader

2. John Egerton, *Speak Now Against the Day.* New York: Knopf, 1994, p. 31.

3. Quoted in Clayborne Carson et al., eds., Garrow, Gerald Gill, Vincent Harding, Darlene Clark Hine, *Eyes on the Prize Civil Rights Reader.* New York: Penguin Books, 1991, p. 7.

4. Quoted in Michael D. Davis and Hunter R. Clark, *Thurgood Marshall: Warrior at the Bar, Rebel on the Bench.* New York: Carol Publishing Group, 1992, p. 31

5. Quoted in Lisa Aldred, *Thurgood Marshall: Supreme Court Justice.* New York: Chelsea House, 1990, p. 24.

6. Quoted in Randall W. Bland, *Private Pressure on Public Law: The Legal Career of Justice Thurgood Marshall.* Port Washington, NY: Kennikat Press, 1973, p. 5.

7. Quoted in Aldred, *Thurgood Marshall,* p. 29.

8. Quoted in Davis and Clark, *Thurgood Marshall,* p. 44.

9. Quoted in Davis and Clark, *Thurgood Marshall,* p. 45.

10. Quoted in Carl T. Rowan, *Dream Makers, Dream Breakers: The World of Justice Thurgood Marshall,* Boston: Little, Brown, 1993, p. 45.

Chapter 2: Finding a Calling

11. Quoted in Mark V. Tushnet, *Making Civil Rights Law: Thurgood Marshall and the Supreme Court, 1936–1961.* New York: Oxford University Press, 1994, p. 68.

12. Quoted in Sanford Wexler, *The Civil Rights Movement: An Eyewitness History.* New York: Facts On File, 1993, p. 30.

13. Quoted in Rowan, *Dream Makers, Dream Breakers,* pp. 46–47.

14. Quoted in Davis and Clark, *Thurgood Marshall,* p. 55.

15. Quoted in Debra Hess, *Thurgood Marshall: The Fight for Equal Justice.* Englewood Cliffs, NJ: Silver Burdett, 1990, pp. 30–31.

16. Quoted in Hess, *Thurgood Marshall,* p. 35.

17. Quoted in Davis and Clark, *Thurgood Marshall,* p. 70.

18. Quoted in Tushnet, *Making Civil Rights Law,* p. 10.

19. Quoted in Roger Goldman, with David Gallen, *Thurgood Marshall: Justice for All.* New York: Carroll and Graf, 1992, p. 39.

20. Quoted in James Haskins, *Thurgood Marshall: A Life for Justice.* New York: Henry Holt, 1992, p. 35.

21. Quoted in Tushnet, *Making Civil Rights Law,* p. 11.

22. Quoted in Tushnet, *Making Civil Rights Law,* p. 14.

23. Quoted in Davis and Clark, *Thurgood Marshall,* p. 88.

24. Quoted in Davis and Clark, *Thurgood Marshall,* p. 89.

25. Quoted in Hess, *Thurgood Marshall,* p. 39.

26. Quoted in Davis and Clark, *Thurgood Marshall,* p. 98.

27. Quoted in Tushnet, *Making Civil Rights Law,* p. 19.

Chapter 3: On the Road for the NAACP

28. Quoted in Davis and Clark, *Thurgood Marshall,* p. 56.

29. Quoted in Haskins, *Thurgood Marshall*, p. 47.

30. Quoted in Rowan, *Dream Makers, Dream Breakers*, p. 73.

31. Quoted in Rowan, *Dream Makers, Dream Breakers*, p. 73.

32. Quoted in Rowan, *Dream Makers, Dream Breakers*, p. 74.

33. Quoted in Richard Kluger, *Simple Justice.* New York: Knopf, 1976, p. 204.

34. Quoted in Rowan, *Dream Makers, Dream Breakers*, p. 77.

35. Quoted in Davis and Clark, *Thurgood Marshall*, p. 94.

36. Quoted in Rowan, *Dream Makers, Dream Breakers*, p. 78.

37. Quoted in Rowan, *Dream Makers, Dream Breakers*, p. 76.

38. Quoted in Rowan, *Dream Makers, Dream Breakers*, p. 76.

39. Quoted in Davis and Clark, *Thurgood Marshall*, p. 108.

40. Quoted in Davis and Clark, *Thurgood Marshall*, p. 108.

41. Quoted in Davis and Clark, *Thurgood Marshall*, p. 110.

42. Quoted in Davis and Clark, *Thurgood Marshall*, p. 11.

43. Quoted in Davis and Clark, *Thurgood Marshall*, p. 142.

44. Quoted in Hess, *Thurgood Marshall*, p. 50.

45. Quoted in Davis and Clark, *Thurgood Marshall*, p. 118.

Chapter 4: Taking On the Military

46. Quoted in Rowan, *Dream Makers, Dream Breakers*, p. 79.

47. Egerton, *Speak Now Against the Day*, p. 211.

48. Quoted in Nancy Whitelaw, *Mr. Civil Rights: The Story of Thurgood Marshall.* Greensboro, NC: Morgan Reynolds, 1995, p. 44.

49. Quoted in Rowan, *Dream Makers, Dream Breakers*, p. 102.

50. Quoted in Haskins, *Thurgood Marshall*, p. 77.

51. Quoted in Egerton, *Speak Now Against the Day*, p. 415.

52. Quoted in Haskins, *Thurgood Marshall*, p. 78.

53. Quoted in Egerton, *Speak Now Against the Day*, p. 415.

54. Quoted in Goldman, *Thurgood Marshall*, p. 114.

55. Quoted in Davis and Clark, *Thurgood Marshall*, p. 128.

56. Quoted in Davis and Clark, *Thurgood Marshall*, p. 130.

57. Quoted in Davis and Clark, *Thurgood Marshall*, p. 126.

58. Quoted in Davis and Clark, *Thurgood Marshall*, p. 130.

59. Quoted in Davis and Clark, *Thurgood Marshall*, p. 132.

60. Quoted in Rowan, *Dream Makers, Dream Breakers*, p. 169.

Chapter 5: The Beginning of the End

61. Quoted in Davis and Clark, *Thurgood Marshall*, p. 143.

62. Quoted in Davis and Clark, *Thurgood Marshall*, p. 146.

63. Quoted in Davis and Clark, *Thurgood Marshall*, p. 146.

64. Quoted in Egerton, *Speak Now Against the Day*, p. 592.

65. Quoted in Rowan, *Dream Makers, Dream Breakers*, pp. 9–10.

66. Quoted in Rowan, *Dream Makers, Dream Breakers*, p. 10.

67. Quoted in Rowan, *Dream Makers, Dream Breakers*, pp. 16–17.

68. Quoted in Kenneth W. Goings, *The NAACP Comes of Age: The Defeat of Judge John J.*

Parker. Indianapolis: Indiana University Press, 1990, p. 83.

Chapter 6: Ending School Segregation

69. Quoted in Rowan, *Dream Makers, Dream Breakers,* p. 190.

70. Quoted in Davis and Clark, *Thurgood Marshall,* p. 173.

71. Quoted in Rowan, *Dream Makers, Dream Breakers,* pp. 199–200.

72. Quoted in Tushnet, *Making Civil Rights Law,* p. 179.

73. Quoted in Rowan, *Dream Makers, Dream Breakers,* p. 200.

74. Quoted in John P. MacKenzie et al., eds., *The Justices of the United States Supreme Court, 1789–1969: Their Lives and Major Opinions,* vol. 4. New York: Chelsea House and R. R. Bowker, 1969, pp. 3074–75.

75. Quoted in Lewis H. Fenderson, *Thurgood Marshall: Fighter for Justice.* New York: McGraw-Hill, 1972, p. 100.

76. Quoted in Rowan, *Dream Makers, Dream Breakers,* p. 200.

77. Quoted in Haskins, *Thurgood Marshall,* pp. 92–93.

78. Quoted in Marjorie G. Fribourg, *The Supreme Court in American History: Ten Great Decisions.* Philadelphia: Macrae Smith, 1965, pp. 139–40.

79. Quoted in Bernard Schwartz, *A History of the Supreme Court.* New York: Oxford University Press, 1993, pp. 306–307.

80. Quoted in Schwartz, *A History of the Supreme Court,* pp. 286, 306–307.

81. Quoted in Egerton, *Speak Now Against The Day,* p. 608.

82. Quoted in Schwartz, *A History of the Supreme Court,* pp. 306–307.

83. Quoted in Wexler, *The Civil Rights Movement,* p. 48.

84. Quoted in Egerton, *Speak Now Against the Day,* p. 610.

85. Quoted in Egerton, *Speak Now Against the Day,* p. 610.

86. Quoted in Egerton, *Speak Now Against the Day,* p. 609.

87. Quoted in Egerton, *Speak Now Against the Day,* p. 617.

88. Quoted in Egerton, *Speak Now Against the Day,* pp. 617–18.

89. Quoted in Rowan, *Dream Makers, Dream Breakers,* p. 225.

90. Quoted in Henry Hampton and Steve Fayer, *Voices of Freedom: An Oral History of the Civil Rights Movement from the 1950s Through the 1980s.* New York: Bantam Books, 1990, p. 47.

91. Quoted in Whitelaw, *Mr. Civil Rights,* p. 74.

92. Quoted in Wexler, *The Civil Rights Movement,* p. 105.

93. Quoted in Schwartz, *A History of the Supreme Court,* p. 308.

Chapter 7: Marshall on the Bench

94. Quoted in Tushnet, *Making Civil Rights Law,* p. 301.

95. Quoted in Rowan, *Dream Makers, Dream Breakers,* p. 283.

96. Quoted in MacKenzie, *Justices of the United States Supreme Court 1789–1969,* p. 3082.

97. Quoted in Rowan, *Dream Makers, Dream Breakers,* pp. 287–88.

98. Quoted in Haskins, *Thurgood Marshall,* pp. 124–25.

99. Quoted in MacKenzie, *The Justices of the United States Supreme Court 1789–1969,* p. 3083.

100. Quoted in Bland, *Private Pressure on Public Law,* p. 151.

101. Quoted in Davis and Clark, *Thurgood Marshall,* p. 275.

102. Quoted in Bland, *Private Pressure on Public Law,* p. 152.

103. Quoted in Haskins, *Thurgood Marshall,* p. 132.

104. Quoted in Davis and Clark, *Thurgood Marshall*, p. 273.

105. Quoted in Davis and Clark, *Thurgood Marshall*, p. 275.

106. Quoted in Davis and Clark, *Thurgood Marshall*, p. 271.

107. Quoted in Davis and Clark, *Thurgood Marshall*, p. 275.

108. Quoted in Rowan, *Dream Makers, Dream Breakers*, p. 299.

109. Quoted in Haskins, *Thurgood Marshall*, pp. 144–45.

Chapter 8: The Supreme Court Years

110. Quoted in Bob Woodward and Scott Armstrong, *The Brethren: Inside the Supreme Court*. New York: Simon & Schuster, 1979, p. 194.

111. Quoted in Goldman, *Thurgood Marshall*, p. 268.

112. Quoted in Bland, *Private Pressure on Public Law*, p. 164.

113. Quoted in Woodward and Armstrong, *The Brethren*, p. 195.

114. Quoted in Goldman, *Thurgood Marshall*, p. 243.

115. Quoted in Goldman, *Thurgood Marshall*, pp. 230–31.

116. Quoted in Roger Goldman, with David Gallen, *Justice William J. Brennan, Jr.: Freedom First*. New York: Carroll and Graf, 1994, p. 21.

117. Quoted in Woodward and Armstrong, *The Brethren*, p. 47.

118. Quoted in Goldman, *Thurgood Marshall*, p. 213.

119. Quoted in Goldman, *Thurgood Marshall*, pp. 214–15.

120. Quoted in Davis and Clark, *Thurgood Marshall*, p. 282.

121. Quoted in Goldman, *Thurgood Marshall*, p. 222.

122. Quoted in Charles P. Cozic, ed., *Civil Liberties: Opposing Viewpoints*. San Diego: Greenhaven Press, 1994, p. 210.

123. Quoted in Haskins, *Thurgood Marshall*, p. 139.

124. Quoted in Haskins, *Thurgood Marshall*, p. 144.

125. Quoted in Haskins, *Thurgood Marshall*, p. 146.

126. Quoted in Davis and Clark, *Thurgood Marshall*, p. 10.

127. Quoted in Rowan, *Dream Makers, Dream Breakers*, p. 406.

128. Quoted in Goldman, *Thurgood Marshall*, p. 171.

129. Quoted in Davis and Clark, *Thurgood Marshall*, p. 369.

Chapter 9: The Marshall Legacy

130. Rowan, *Dream Makers, Dream Breakers*, p. 3.

131. Quoted in Rowan, *Dream Makers, Dream Breakers*, p. 452.

132. Quoted in Paul Dugan, "Mourners Reflect Breadth of Marshall Legacy," *Washington Post*, January 28, 1993, p. A1.

133. Quoted in Goldman, *Thurgood Marshall*, p. 14.

134. Quoted in Wexler, *The Civil Rights Movement*, p. 266.

135. Quoted in Dugan, "Mourners Reflect Breadth of Marshall Legacy," p. A1.

136. Quoted in Lynne Duke, "Funeral for Civil Rights Warrior Rings with Recommitment," *Washington Post*, January 29, 1993, p. A14.

137. Quoted in Davis and Clark, *Thurgood Marshall*, p. 382.

138. Quoted in Rowan, *Dream Makers, Dream Breakers*, p. 453.

For Further Reading

Lisa Aldred, *Thurgood Marshall: Supreme Court Justice.* New York: Chelsea House, 1990. Biography of Thurgood Marshall. An in-depth and lively look at the life of Marshall complete with personal insights and anecdotes.

Lewis H. Fenderson, *Thurgood Marshall: Fighter for Justice.* New York: McGraw-Hill, 1972. Biography that emphasizes Marshall's contribution to black civil rights.

Debra Hess, *Thurgood Marshall: The Fight for Equal Justice.* Englewood Cliffs, NJ: Silver Burdett, 1990. Biography that concentrates on Marshall's role in the Civil Rights Movement. This book provides an easy-to-understand introduction to the overall Civil Rights Movement.

Don Lawson, *The Changing Face of the Constitution.* New York: Franklin Watts, 1979. Outlines the Constitution and highlights its changing interpretation in response to the needs of the American people.

John P. MacKenzie et al., eds., *The Justices of the United States Supreme Court, 1789–1969: Their Lives and Major Opinions,* vol. 4. New York: Chelsea House and R. R. Bowker, 1969. Historical overview of the U.S. Supreme Court. This book provides an in-depth look at the Supreme Court and how the decisions of the Court have shaped our lives.

Fred Powledge, *We Shall Overcome: Heroes of the Civil Rights Movement.* New York: Charles Scribner's Sons, 1993. Stories of the leaders of the Civil Rights Movement. This book provides a personal look at the struggle for civil rights as told by those who participated in the movement.

Rosemary C. Salomone, *Equal Education Under Law.* New York: St. Martin's Press, 1986. Salomone's book provides a historical look at school desegregation and the struggle for equal education in the United States.

David G. Savage, *Turning Right: The Making of the Rehnquist Supreme Court.* New York: Wiley, 1992. A history of the U.S. Supreme Court under Chief Justice Rehnquist.

J. Harvie Wilkinson III, *From Brown to Bakke: The Supreme Court and School Integration, 1954–1978.* New York: Oxford University Press, 1979. Focuses on the Court's decisions on school desegregation and the issue of reverse discrimination.

Works Consulted

Steven Anzovin and Janet Podell, eds., *The U.S. Constitution and the Supreme Court.* New York: H. W. Wilson, 1988. Reprints of articles, essays, and book excerpts discussing the Constitution.

Lerone Bennett Jr., *Before the Mayflower: A History of Black America.* Chicago: Johnson's Publishing, 1987. Historical overview of African Americans in the United States.

Joan Biskupic, "Thurgood Marshall, Retired Justice, Dies, Unyielding Defender of Individual Rights," the *Washington Post,* January 25, 1993. A newspaper account of Marshall's legacy.

Randall W. Bland, *Private Pressure on Public Law: The Legal Career of Justice Thurgood Marshall.* Port Washington, NY: Kennikat Press, 1973. Examines the impact of Thurgood Marshall from his days as director-counsel for the NAACP to his years as Justice Marshall of the Supreme Court.

Clayborne Carson et al., eds., *Eyes on the Prize Civil Rights Reader.* New York: Penguin Books, 1991. Contains documents, speeches, and first-person accounts of the Civil Rights Movement from 1954 to 1990.

Michael D. Davis and Hunter R. Clark, *Thurgood Marshall: Warrior at the Bar, Rebel on the Bench.* New York: Carol Publishing Group, 1992. Biography examines Marshall's views on abortion, capital punishment, women's rights, and affirmative action.

Paul Dugan, "Mourners Reflect Breadth of Marshall Legacy," the *Washington Post,* January 28, 1993. A newspaper account of Marshall's funeral with firsthand reports of those who participated in the service.

Lynne Duke, "Funeral for Civil Rights Warrior Rings with Recommitment," the *Washington Post,* January 29, 1993. A newspaper account of Marshall's funeral.

John Egerton, *Speak Now Against the Day.* New York: Knopf, 1994. A history of the Civil Rights Movement told through first-person narratives set within the context of social events.

Marjorie G. Fribourg, *The Supreme Court in American History: Ten Great Decisions.* Philadelphia: Macrae Smith, 1965. Discussion of ten landmark decisions of the Supreme Court, focusing on the people, politics, and issues involved.

Roger Goldman, with David Gallen, *Thurgood Marshall: Justice For All.* New York: Carroll and Graf, 1992. Includes recollections of those who worked with Marshall, as well as a selection of his opinions and dissents as a Supreme Court justice. This book offers a personal view of Marshall the man as seen by his peers.

Kenneth W. Goings, *The NAACP Comes of Age: The Defeat of Judge John J. Parker.* Indianapolis: Indiana University Press, 1990. Explores the development of the NAACP into a powerful organization and its major role in the defeat of confirmation of Judge John J. Parker to the Supreme Court.

Henry Hampton and Steve Fayer, *Voices of Freedom: An Oral History of the Civil Rights Movement from the 1950s Through the 1980s.* New York: Bantam Books, 1990. An oral history of the Civil Rights Movement as told through first-person narratives of the leading activists of the Civil Rights Movement.

Maureen Harrison and Steve Gilbert, eds., *Landmark Decisions of the United States Supreme Court.* Beverly Hills, CA: Excellent Books, 1991. An overview of landmark court cases reviewed by the U.S. Supreme Court.

James Haskins, *Thurgood Marshall: A Life for Justice.* New York: Henry Holt, 1992. Examines the life and accomplishments of the first black judge to be appointed to the Supreme Court. This book focuses on Marshall's commitment to the fight for winning civil rights for all Americans and how this commitment shaped his life.

D. J. Herda, *Thurgood Marshall: Civil Rights Champion.* Springfield, NJ: Enslow, 1995. Biographical history of Thurgood Marshall, as part of the *Justices of the Supreme Court* series.

Richard Kluger, *Simple Justice.* New York: Knopf, 1976. This books examines the issue of segregation in education, its impact on society, and the legislation that helped in desegregation.

Roy M. Mersky and J. Myron Jacobstein, eds., *The Supreme Court of the United States: Hearings and Reports on Successful and Unsuccessful Nominations of Supreme Court Justices by the Senate Judiciary Committee, 1916–1975.* New York: William S. Hein, 1977. Minutes and reports from the Senate subcommittee on U.S. Supreme Court nominations.

Donald G. Nieman, *Promises to Keep: African-Americans and the Constitutional Order, 1776 to the Present.* New York: Oxford University Press, 1991. Traces the relationship of African Americans and the Constitution since 1776 and examines the effects of racism on their lives.

Carl T. Rowan, *Dream Makers, Dream Breakers: The World of Justice Thurgood Marshall.* Boston: Little, Brown, 1993. Biography drawn from NAACP files and exclusive interviews with Marshall.

Bernard Schwartz, *A History of the Supreme Court.* New York: Oxford University Press, 1993. Historical overview of the U.S. Supreme Court system.

Thomas Sowell, *Civil Rights: Rhetoric or Reality.* New York: William Morrow, 1984. Thomas Sowell looks at the state of civil rights of African Americans for the twenty years following the passage of the civil rights Act of 1964. This book objectively examines the question of whether civil rights have been obtained for African Americans.

Subcommittee of the Committee on the Judiciary, United States Senate, *Nomination of Thurgood Marshall to Be Solicitor General of the United States.* Washington, DC: U.S. Government Printing Office. Minutes from the Senate subcommittee on the nomination of Thurgood Marshall to be solicitor general of the United States.

Mark V. Tushnet, *Making Civil Rights Law: Thurgood Marshall and the Supreme Court, 1936–1961.* New York: Oxford University Press, 1994. A history of Marshall's civil rights battles while head of the NAACP's legal defense fund.

Sanford Wexler, *The Civil Rights Movement: An Eyewitness History.* New York: Facts On File, 1993. History of the Civil Rights Movement in the United States.

Nancy Whitelaw, *Mr. Civil Rights: The Story of Thurgood Marshall.* Greensboro, NC: Morgan Reynolds, 1995. Biography of Marshall, with emphasis on his Supreme Court career.

Bob Woodward and Scott Armstrong, *The Brethren: Inside the Supreme Court.* New York: Simon & Schuster, 1979. A look at the daily life and political maneuvering inside the U.S. Supreme Court.

Index

racism, 16–17
  see also discrimination;
    segregation
Reagan, Ronald, 88–89
Redfield, Robert, 50
Reed, Stanley F., 58, 61, 62
Rehnquist, William H., 86,
  97
Ryan, William, 76

segregation, 11–12, 15
  effects of, 50, 61, 64
  in accommodations, 18,
    26, 89
  in education, 17, 19, 61,
    62
    Brown decision (text),
      64
    Briggs case, 53–54
    Gaines case, 32–36
    McLaurin case, 51–52
    Murray case, 27–30
  in employment, 11–12
  in the armed forces,
    41–49
  legal basis of, 26–27, 39,
    52–53
  psychological effects of,
    55–56, 64
  sociological basis for, 50
  see also under NAACP
separate-but-equal doctrine,
  44, 71
  in education, 50–55, 57,
    62, 64
  Marshall on, 39
  NAACP plan to attack,
    52–57
  Plessy v. Ferguson, 26–27
solicitor general, 73
Stanley v. Georgia, 84

Stewart, Potter, 83
Sweatt v. Painter, 50, 51–52,
  64

Talmadge, Herman, 65
Timmerman, George, 53
To Secure These Rights (civil
  rights commission), 44
Truman, Harry, 44
Tuskegee Institute, 43

United States
  armed forces, 41–49
  Constitution, 22
    Eighth Amendment, 85
    First Amendment,
      83–84
    Fourteenth Amend-
      ment, 16, 26, 33,
      50–51, 56, 86
    Fourth Amendment,
      84, 87–88
    importance to Marshall,
      15–16, 81–82, 91
  Supreme Court, 93
    accommodations cases,
      26
    capital punishment
      cases, 85
    desegregation guide-
      lines of, 65–66
    education cases, 35,
      51–52, 58–64, 68,
      70, 88
      Brown v. Board of
        Education, 58–64
      Cooper v. Aaron, 68, 70
      Lloyd L. Gaines v.
        S.W. Canada Regis-
        trar, U. of Mo., 35
      Milliken v. Bradley, 88

Sweatt v. Painter,
  51–52
freedom of expression
  cases, 83–84
justices, 26, 58, 61–63,
  83, 85–86
  see also individual
    justices
rights of the accused
  cases, 87
rights of the poor
  cases, 86–87
search and seizure
  cases, 84, 87–88
United States v. Kras, 86–87
University of Maryland
  Law School, 19, 27–29
University of Missouri Law
  School, 32–36
University of Oklahoma,
  51–52
University of Texas Law
  School, 50

Villard, Oswald, 15
Vinson, Fred M., 58, 61
Voices of Freedom, 42

Waring, J. Waties, 53, 57
Warren, Earl, 61, 62, 63,
  86
  Court of, 61–66, 71,
    83–86
Wells-Barnett, Ida B., 12,
  13
White, Walter, 26, 49, 55,
  67
  opinion of Marshall, 24
Williams, Isaiah (grand-
  father), 13–14
World War II, 41–44

Picture Credits

Cover photo: Archive Photos
AP/Wide World Photos, 59, 63, 66, 67, 68, 79, 83, 92, 96
Archive Photos, 87
Consolidated News/Archive Photos, 85
Courtesy of Cecilia S. Marshall, 14 (both), 16, 73, 90
Library of Congress, 12, 18, 22, 23, 25, 27, 36, 54 (both), 56, 70, 89, 98
Lincoln University, 17
National Archives, 41, 44, 45, 47, 49
Shomburg Center for Research in Black Culture, 11, 29, 32, 35, 58, 65
UPI/Bettmann, 43, 75, 77, 78, 81
UPI/Corbis-Bettmann, 9, 20, 33, 52, 60, 69, 72

About the Authors

Deborah Hitzeroth is a Virginia-based writer with a background in journalism and travel. She received a B.A. in journalism from the University of Missouri before working as a reporter and editor in Texas and San Diego. This is her seventh book.

Sharon Leon is a Texas-based writer with a background in business and technology. She received a B.S. from the University of Missouri before moving to Texas and working on technical publications. This is her fourth book.